Asher Benjamin (1773–1845)

THE
AMERICAN BUILDER'S COMPANION

OR, A

SYSTEM OF ARCHITECTURE
PARTICULARLY ADAPTED TO THE PRESENT
STYLE OF BUILDING

BY

ASHER BENJAMIN

an unabridged reprint of the sixth edition
with 70 plates
and a new introduction by
William Morgan

DOVER PUBLICATIONS, INC., NEW YORK

Published in Canada by General Publishing Company, Ltd., 30 Lesmill Road, Don Mills, Toronto, Ontario.
Published in the United Kingdom by Constable and Company, Ltd.

This Dover edition, first published in 1969, is an unabridged republication of the sixth (1827) edition, as published by R. P. & C. Williams.
This reprint also contains a new introduction by William Morgan.

Standard Book Number: 486-22236-5
Library of Congress Catalog Card Number: 68–58318

Manufactured in the United States of America
Dover Publications, Inc.
180 Varick Street
New York, N. Y. 10014

INTRODUCTION

THE architecture of the first forty years of the nineteenth century has been vaguely called "Anglo-Greco-Roman" in England, but perhaps a better term for this period in America, especially until 1830, would be "Federal Neo-Classic." Charles Bulfinch was the dominant architectural force in post-Revolutionary Boston and it was Bulfinch who, thoroughly taken by the work of Robert and James Adam, introduced the Federal-Adamesque style into Boston upon his return from England in 1787. Bulfinch transformed Boston from a provincial capital into an urbane and elegant city. Drawing his inspiration from the brothers Adam, James Gibbs, and Sir William Chambers, and ignoring the more progressive work he had seen in France (and which served as a source for more avant-garde architects such as Thomas Jefferson and Benjamin Latrobe), Bulfinch correctly adjudged the conservative and still English-oriented taste of Boston and filled the city with his version of the Adamesque.

New England was enjoying a period of unprecedented prosperity, and Boston, rivaled only by Philadelphia, was the artistic and cultural center of the nation. Asher Benjamin was one of several young architects who were attracted to Boston around this time. (Alexander Parris, Isaiah Rogers, and Solomon Willard were some of the other men who were to play a role in the burgeoning growth of the city.) It was only natural that these architects should have imitated the work of Bulfinch, and Benjamin, whose *American Builder's Companion* of 1806 included a number of Bulfinch inspired designs, was no exception.

Asher Benjamin was born in Hartland, Connecticut, about 1773 and received his early training from a local builder. The first thirty years of his life were spent in the Connecticut River Valley, where he built houses in Greenfield, Massachusetts, and

v

Suffield, Connecticut; a school building in Deerfield; and a church in Northampton, Massachusetts. Benjamin also lived in Windsor, Vermont, and is credited with at least two houses and a church in that community. By 1803 he was living in Boston and was listed in the city directory as a "housewright."

In Boston Benjamin built a number of houses in the Bulfinch manner which contributed to the restrained red brick elegance of Beacon Hill. The twin houses at 54 and 55 Beacon Street, opposite Boston Common, with their gently bowed fronts, delicate iron balconies, pilasters, and doorways flanked with slender sidelights and topped with semi-circular fanlights remain as examples of Benjamin's work, as does the range of houses (including his own) on West Cedar Street. Benjamin also designed two churches in Boston which survive, the West Church built in 1806 and the Charles Street Meetinghouse of 1807. Although basically similar to earlier Bulfinch churches (such as the Church of the Holy Cross), particularly in their belfried clock towers, they are superb pieces of architecture in their own right. Benjamin executed other buildings outside of Boston, including the Rhode Island Union Bank in Newport, which, before its recent demolition, was one of that city's finest public buildings.

Although these buildings show him to be a competent architect, Asher Benjamin's real contribution to American architecture was his seven handbooks or builder's guides. The first book on architecture printed in America was Abraham Swan's *British Architect: or, the Builder's Treasury of Staircases*, published in Philadelphia in 1775, but the work was merely a reprint of an earlier London edition of 1745. The first original American architectural work was Benjamin's *The Country Builder's Assistant: Containing a Collection of New Designs of Carpentry and Architecture*, published in Greenfield in 1797, twenty-two years after the *British Architect*. *The Country Builder's Assistant* was the first of several books on architecture that altogether ran to forty-four editions and which profoundly influenced the architecture of New England in the early nineteenth century.

In addition to *The Country Builder's Assistant*, Benjamin wrote *The American Builder's Companion* (1806 and following), *The Rudiments of Architecture* (first published in 1814), *The Practical House Carpenter* (1830), *The Practice of Architecture* (1833), *The Builder's Guide* (1839), and *The Elements of Architecture* (1843). Of these, *The Practical House Carpenter* was the most popular, although each book was published in several editions. Architectural books had had an effect on pre-Revolutionary American architecture, but Asher Benjamin's books were designed specifically for the American builder. In an age which marks the infancy of the architectural profession (Benjamin was one of the men who formed the American Institution of Architects in 1837, the predecessor of the American Institute of Architects), these books served as the only architectural education for carpenter-builders throughout New England. Benjamin's publications contained basic designs and practical instruction on the construction of elementary structural and geometric forms, but more importantly, they spread the Bulfinch-Benjamin interpretation of the Adamesque to the countryside beyond Boston. That plates from Benjamin's books were the inspiration for many Northern New England houses and churches is borne out by numerous Federal style buildings along the Maine coast and in the river valleys of New Hampshire and Vermont. Long believed to have been designed by Bulfinch, the elegant row of Federal houses in Orford, New Hampshire, were, in all likelihood, the work of a local builder who used one of Benjamin's books for a guide. Drawings made by Alexander Parris in 1807 for a church in Portland suggest that Parris may have freely borrowed a church design from the first edition of Benjamin's *The American Builder's Companion*; Plate 33 of *The Country Builder's Assistant* was the design used by Vermont builder Lavius Fillmore in his first Congregational Church in Bennington in 1806.

As the Bennington Church illustrates, Benjamin leaned somewhat on English sources such as James Gibbs' *Book of Architecture*, and in the preface to the third edition of *The American Builder's Companion* he acknowledged his indebtedness "to Sir William Chambers' incomparable Treatise on Civil Architecture" and "to P. Nicholson's excellent books." But Benjamin relied on tried designs only in so much as the conservative nature of his rural carpenter-builder consumers demanded. He added new plates and details in subsequent editions of his books and by 1827 the sixth and final edition of *The American Builder's Companion* offered the "Grecian architecture" that was replacing the Federal style. This edition included the "Doric Order of the Temple of Minerva, at Athens, called Parthenon," and the "Ionic Temple on the River Ilissus, at Athens," as well as a comparison of the Greek and Roman Doric.

The American Builder's Companion; or, A New System of Architecture Particularly Adapted to the Present Style of Building in the United States of America, was first published in Boston in 1806 by Etheridge and Bliss. This second work of Benjamin's was jointly authored with stucco worker Daniel Raynerd, however, Raynerd sold his rights to the book before the second edition, published by Samuel Etheridge, Jr., in Charlestown, appeared in 1811. The third, fourth, fifth, and sixth editions were published by R. P. and C. Williams in Boston in 1816, 1820, 1826, and 1827 respectively. The sixth and last edition, as the result of continual revision and refinement, is certainly of the greatest general interest. Three church designs in the sixth edition illustrate the range of the work. Plate 56 is a design for a church in the Gibbsian manner with a pedimented, projecting pavilion; there is the standard New England "Colonial" steeple with square and octagonal stages and topped with a weather vane. Plate 57 is a plan and elevation of Benjamin's Federal style West Church, while Plate K offers a church design, which although Georgian in plan, has a Greek Doric temple-form porch.

The present reprint of the sixth edition of *The American Builder's Companion* makes available the text and illustrations of this influential work which set the standard in early nineteenth-century New England architecture. Not only does this edition illustrate various Georgian and Federal designs for a variety of building types and interior details, but it also offers practical guidelines for the untrained architect on how to construct basic geometrical forms in wood, such as "how a Scroll is to be got out of the Solid" or how "To draw the Ionic volute," or "a form in which a roof may be framed," and even offers advice of a philosophical nature. For example: "In sacred places all obscene, grotesque, and heathenish representations ought to be avoided; for indecent fables, extravagent conceits, or instruments and symbols of pagan worship are very improper ornaments in structures consecrated to christian (sic) devotion." Most importantly, the book, in covering a span of twenty years, serves as an excellent barometer of the taste of the period. *The American Builder's Companion* included late Georgian details from English books, it codified and made available to the country builder Bulfinch's version of the Adamesque, it offered Neo-Classic Roman stylistic devices, such as urns, friezes, and fireplace moldings, and it had grown to encompass the Greek Revival, placing the ancient monuments at the disposal of un-travelled builders. It may be argued that dependence on the book by rural architects led to a precious and overwrought development of the Federal style, but in so doing, it insured a high degree of design competence and stylistic sophistication that might not have otherwise occured. It is also conceivable that without books such as *The American Builder's Companion* and *The Practical House Carpenter* the Greek Revival would not have gained such widespread acceptance. *The American Builder's Companion* mirrored its author's flexibility toward changes in taste and his lack of insistence on any particular style. Throughout his publications Benjamin encouraged a certain freedom of interpretation and common sense among his readers. In the preface to the third edition, he defends his alteration of the time-honored diameter-height ratios of the Orders: "Experience has taught me that no determinate rule for columns, in all situations, will answer." In the preface to the fifth edition he states:

> Being the first who have for a great length of time published any New System of Architecture, we do not expect to escape some degree of censure. Old fashioned workmen, who have for many years followed the footsteps of Palladio and Langley, will no doubt, leave their old path with reluctance. But as impressed as we are, with a conviction that reform in some parts of the system of Architecture is loudly demanded, and feeling a confidence from our knowledge of theory, . . . we have ventured, without the aid of subscription, to exhibit our work to public view.

This pragmatic approach to building was disseminated by the books of Asher Benjamin and contributed to an inventiveness and variety which gave strength and greatness to nineteenth-century American architecture.

Washington, D. C.
August, 1968

WILLIAM MORGAN

THE

AMERICAN BUILDER'S COMPANION;

OR, A

SYSTEM OF ARCHITECTURE,

PARTICULARLY ADAPTED

TO THE PRESENT STYLE OF BUILDING.

TREATING

ON PRACTICAL GEOMETRY;
THE ORIGIN OF BUILDING.
OF THE FIVE ORDERS OF ARCHITECTURE; OF
THEIR PARTICULAR PARTS AND EMBELLISH-
MENTS, AND OF THEIR APPLICATION.
ALSO, VERY FULLY ON STAIRS.

ON PLANS AND ELEVATIONS OF HOUSES.....FOR BOTH
TOWN AND COUNTRY.
ON CHURCHES.........COURT HOUSES, &c.
ON SASHES....SASH FRAMES. ...SHUTTERS.....DOORS
.....CORNICES.... BASE AND SURBASE MOULD-
INGS.....ARCHITRAVES, &c.

ILLUSTRATED WITH

SEVENTY COPPERPLATE ENGRAVINGS.

Sixth Edition....Corrected and Enlarged.

WITH A PLAN AND ELEVATIONS OF A CHURCH, AND NINE ADDITIONAL PLATES, ON
HANDRAILS FOR CIRCULAR STAIRS, AND

GRECIAN ARCHITECTURE.

BY ASHER BENJAMIN,

ARCHITECT AND CARPENTER.

Boston:

PUBLISHED BY R. P. & C. WILLIAMS....CORNHILL SQUARE;

No. 79, Washington Street, opposite the Old State House.

DUTTON & WENTWORTH, PRINTERS.

1827.

PREFACE,

TO THE THIRD EDITION.

FIVE years having elapsed since the first publication of the American Builder ; during which time I have been constantly employed in drawing and executing plans for buildings. The experience of that time enables me to confirm some, and reject other former methods.

Sixteen plates, which were in the first edition, I have laid aside, and have added twenty-nine new ones ; which almost make this a new work.

I have first laid down and explained such problems in Geometry, as are absolutely necessary to the well understanding of the subject. I have next treated on the origin of building, of mouldings, and of the orders. I have endeavoured to explain them so clearly and fully, that they cannot be misunderstood. At first they were selected from several authors, drawn at large, and wrought. After careful examination, such parts as I did not approve, were altered, by drawing and working them over again, and repeating this process several times, till after the most minute and careful examination of every part of the four first orders, I was confirmed in the opinion, that no further alterations for the better could be made ; for the result of which experiments see these orders as they are severally laid down.

I have given the Tuscan column eight diameters in height, in imitation of the Trajan and Antonian columns at Rome, which are of that height, and reckoned of the Tuscan order ; and have regularly progressed, by giving the Doric nine, the Ionic ten, the Corinthian and composite eleven diameters each.

I expect it will be said by some, who rigidly adhere to the proportions of the ancients, that the Tuscan column ought not to be but seven, the Doric eight, the Ionic nine, and the Corinthian and Composite ten Diameters each in height.

Experience has taught me that no determinate rule for columns, in all situations, will answer; they must be proportioned according to the weight, or apparent weight they are to sustain. I do not recollect, in the course of seventeen years extensive practice, to have made either of the orders larger than the proportion here given; and in but few cases so large. My principal aim has been directed toward explaining with perspicuity, the foundation of this art; the orders, and their particular parts. For this explanation I am principally indebted to Sir William Chambers's incomparable Treatise on Civil Architecture; how far I have succeeded in my attempt, I must submit to the judgment of others.

I have given examples of sashes, sash frames, and shutters; and how to set them in a brick wall; have also treated fully on stairs; for which, I must acknowledge myself indebted to P. Nicholson's excellent books on that subject.

Several plans and elevations of buildings of different kinds, are to be found in this work, with observations on their several and particular parts.

Note. It may perhaps be asked, why Mr. Raynerd's name, which appeared in the first edition, does not appear in this; I answer, he sold all his right and title to the work soon after its first publication. The plates in this edition, which were drawn and explained by him, have his name affixed to them.

MARCH 1814.

PUBLISHERS' ADVERTISEMENT,

TO THE SIXTH EDITION.

Since the copy right of this work has been transferred to the present proprietors, they have with the advice of the editor and other eminent architects and builders, enlarged this work by additional matter and plates, on Stairs, and on Grecian Doric and Ionic Architecture from the most celebrated remains of antiquity, and an additional plan and elevation for a Meeting-House or Church.

The new plates are numbered alphabetically.

July 1827.

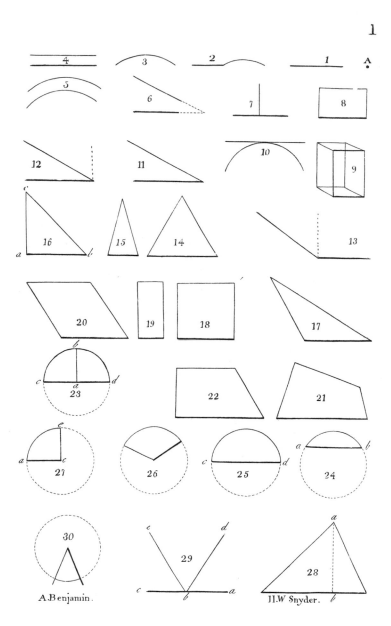

A. Benjamin.

H.W Snyder.

AMERICAN BUILDER'S COMPANION.

PLATE I.

PRACTICAL GEOMETRY.

DEFINITIONS.

GEOMETRY, is that Science which treats of the discriptions and proportions of magnitudes in general.

A point is that which has position, but no magnitude nor dimensions; neither length, breadth, nor thickness, as A.

A right line, is length without breadth or thickness, as 1.

A mixed line, is both right and curved, as 2.

A curve line continually changes its direction between its extreme points, as 3.

Parallel lines are always at the same perpendicular distance; and they never meet though ever so far produced, as 4 and 5.

Oblique right lines change their distance, and would meet, if produced, on the side of the least distance, as 6.

One line is perpendicular to another, when it inclines not more on the one side than the other; or when the angles on both sides of it are equal, as 7.

A surface, or superfices, is an extension, or a figure, but without thickness, as 8.

A body, or solid, is a figure of three dimensions; namely, length, breadth, and thickness, as 9.

A line, or a circle, is tangential, or a tangent to a circle, or other curve, when it touches it without cutting, when both are produced, as 10.

An angle is the inclination, or opening of two lines, having different directions, and meeting in a point, as 11.

A right angle is that which is made by one line perpendicular to another, or when the angle on each side are equal to one another, as the lines a b, and a c, on 16.

An acute angle is less than a right angle, as 12.

An obtuse angle, is greater than a right angle, as 13.

Plain figures that are bound by right lines have names according to the number of their sides, or of their angles; for they have as many sides as angles; the least number being three. A figure of three sides and angles, is called a triangle, as 14, 15, 16, and 17; and they receive particular denominations from the relations of their sides and angles.

An equilateral triangle, is that whose three sides are all equal, as 14.

A right angled triangle, is that which has one right angle, as 16.

An isosceles triangle has only two sides equal, as 15.

A scalene triangle has all sides unequal, as 17.

An obtuse angled triangle has one obtuse angle, as 17.

Of four sided figures their are many sorts; as the square 18, which is a plain regular figure, whose superfices are limited by four equal sides, all at right angles with one another.

The parallelogram 19, receives its name from its opposite sides and ends, being parallel to each other; the parallelogram is also called a long square, or oblong, in consequence of its being longer than it is wide.

The rhomboids 20, is an equilateral parallelogram, whose angles are oblique, as 20.

A trapezium is a quadrilateral, which has neither of its sides parallel, as 21.

A trapezoid hath only one pair of its opposite sides parallel, as 22.

Plane figures having more than four sides are in general called polygons, and receive other particular names, according to the number of their sides or angles.

A pentigon, is a polygon of five sides, as fig. 13, plate 2.

A hexigon, is a polygon of six sides, as fig. 14, plate 2.

A heptagon has seven sides; an octagon eight; a nonagon nine; a decagon ten; an undecagon eleven; and a dodecagon twelve.

A regular polygon has all its sides and its angles equal; and if they are not equal the polygon is irregular.

An equilateral triangle is also a regular figure of three sides, and a square is one of four; the former being called a trigon, and the latter a tetragon.

A circle, is a plain figure, bounded by a curve line, called the circumference, which is every where equidistant from a certain point within, called its centre.

The radius of a circle, is a right line drawn from the centre to the circumference, as *a b*, 23.

A diameter of a circle, is a right line drawn through the centre, terminating on both sides of the circumference, as *c d*, on 23.

An arch of a circle is any part of the circumference, as *a b*, 24.

A chord is a right line joining the extremities of an arch, as *a b*, 24.

A semicircle, is half the circle, or a segment cut off by diameter, as *c d*, 25.

A section, is any part of a circle, bounded by an arch and two radii, drawn to its extremities, as 26.

A quadrant, or quarter of a circle, is a sector, having a quarter of the circumference for its arch, and the two radii are perpendicular to each other, as *c a*, and *o c*, 27.

The measure of any right lined angle, is an arch of any circle contained between the two lines, which form the angle, and the angular point being in the centre, as 30.

The height, or altitude of any figure, as perpendicular let fall from an angle or its vertex to the opposite side, called the base, as the line, *a b*, 28.

When an angle is denoted by three letters, the middle one is the place of the angle, and the other two denote the sides containing that angle ; thus, let *a b d*, be the angle at 29, *b* is the angular point, *a b* and *b d*, are the two sides containing that angle.

PLATE II.

FIG. 1.

To draw a perpendicular to a given point in a line. *a b* is a line, and *d* a given point; take *a* and *b*, two equal distances on each side of *d*, and with your compasses in *a* and *b*, make an intersection at *c*, and draw *c d*, which is the perpendicular required.

FIG. 2.

To erect a perpendicular on the end of a line. Take any point you please above the line, as *c*, and with the distance *c b*, make the arch, *a b d*, and draw the line *a c*, to cut it at *d*, and draw *d b*, the perpendicular.

FIG. 3.

To make a perpendicular with a ten foot rod. Let *b a* be six feet; take eight feet in your compasses; from *b* make the arch *c*, with the distance ten feet from *a*; make the intersection at *c*, and draw the perpendicular, *c b*.

FIG. 4.

To let fall a perpendicular from a given point in a line. In the point *e* make an arch to cross the line *a b*, at *c d*; with the distance *c d*, make the intersection *f*, and draw *e f*, the perpendicular.

FIG. 5.

To divide a line in two equal parts by a perpendicular. In the points *a* and *b*, describe two arches to intersect at *c* and *e*, and draw the line *c e*, which makes the perpendicular required.

FIG. 6.

To erect a perpendicular on the segment of a circle, *a b*. From *i* draw the arch *e d*; and, with the distance, *c d*, and on *c* and *d*, make the intersection *c*, and draw the perpendicular *c i*.

FIG. 7 *and* 10.

An angle being given, to make another equal to it from a point, in a right line. Let *a, c, e*, be the given angle, and *d n*, a right line; *d* the given point;

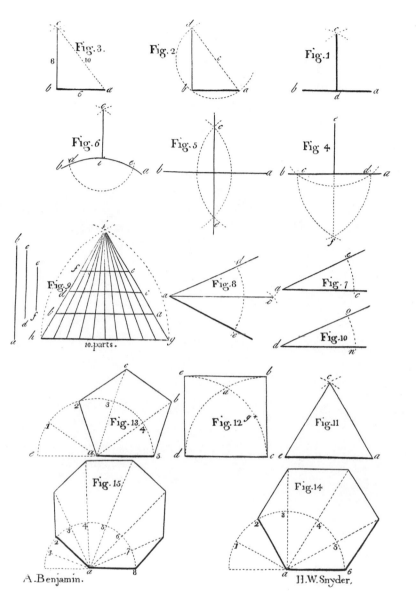

Fig. 3. Fig. 2. Fig. 1.
Fig. 6 Fig. 5 Fig. 4
Fig. 9 Fig. 8 Fig. 7
10. parts. Fig. 10
Fig. 13. Fig. 12 Fig. 11
Fig. 15 Fig. 14

A. Benjamin.   H. W. Snyder.

on a make an arch $c\ e$, with any radius, and on d, with the same radius, describe an arch, $n\ o$; take the opening, $c\ e$, and set it from n to o, and draw $o\ d$, and the angle will be equal to that of a, c, e.

FIG. 8.

To divide any given angle into two equal parts. On a, the angular point, with the radius, $a\ e$, or any other, make the circle $e\ d$; on e and d, with the radius $e\ c$, make the intersection c, and draw the line $c\ a$, which is the division required.

FIG. 9.

To divide a right line given, into any number of equal parts. Let $a\ b$, be a given line, to be divided into ten equal parts ; take any distance in your compasses, more than one tenth of that line, and run them off on the line $h\ g$, and with that distance, make the triangle h, i, g, and draw each tenth division to the angle i ; take the length of the given line $a\ b$, and set one foot of the compasses at a, on the line g, i, and let the other fall on the line $h\ i$, at b, parallel to $h\ g$, and draw the line $a\ b$, which gives the ten divisions required ; the lines $d\ c$, and $f\ e$, or any others which are shorter than the base line of the triangle, can also be drawn across it, which when done, will be divided into tenths.

FIG. 11.

To make an equilateral triangle upon a right line. Take $a\ e$, the given side, in your compasses ; and on a and e, make the intersection c, and draw $a\ c$, and $e\ c$.

FIG. 12.

To make a geometrical square upon a right line. With the given side $d\ c$, and in the points d and c, describe two arches to intersect at a ; divide $a\ c$, into two equal parts at g ; make $a\ e$, and $a\ b$, each equal to $a\ g$, and draw $c\ b$, $d\ e$, and $e\ b$.

FIG. 13, 14, *and* 15.

The sides of any polygon being given to describe the polygon to any number of sides whatever. On the extreme of the given side make a semicircle of any radius, it will be most convenient to make it equal to the side of the polygon ; then divide the semicircle into the same number of equal parts as you would have sides in the polygon, and draw the lines from the centre through the several equal divisions in the semicircle, always omitting the two last, and run the given side round each way upon those lines ; join each side, and it will be completed.

FIG. 13.

How to describe a pentagon. Let *a* 5, be the given side, and continue it out to *e* ; on *a* the centre, describe a semicircle ; divide it into five equal parts ; through 2, 3, and 4, draw *a* 2, *a c*, *a b*, make 5 *b*, equal to *a* 5, 2 *c*, and *c b*, each equal to *a* 5, or *a* 2 ; join *a* 2, 2 *c*, *c b*, and *b* 5 ; in the same way may any polygon be drawn, only divide the semicircle into the same number of parts that the polygon is to have sides.

PLATE III.

FIG. 1.

To make an octagon in a square. Find the centre *n*, with the distance, *a n*, and in the points *a, b, c, d*, make the arches *e n m, l n h, i n f*, and *k n g*; join *l k*, *m i, h g*, and *f e*, which completes the octagon.

FIG. 2.

Any three lines being given to make a triangle. Take one of the given sides, *a b*, and make it the base of the triangle; take the second side, *c a*, in your compasses, place one foot in *a*, and make the arch at *c*; take the third side, *b c*, and place one foot of the compasses in *b*, and make the intersection *c*, then draw *c a*, and *c b*, which completes the triangle.

FIG. 3.

Two right lines being given to find a mean proportion. Join *a c*, and *c b*, in one straight line; divide it into two equal parts at the point *n*, with the radius *n a*, or *n b*; describe a semicircle, and erect the perpendicular *c d*, then is *b c*, to *c d*, as *c d*, is to *c a*.

FIG. 4.

To make a geometrical square, equal to a triangle given. Let *a b n*, be the given triangle; extend *b a*, to *o*; make *a o*, equal to half of *n r*, and with one half of *b o*, on the point *c*, make a semicircle; from *a*, erect a perpendicular intersecting the circle at *f*; make *a d, d e*, and *e f*, each equal to *a f*, and the geometrical square is completed.

FIG. 5.

A tangent line being given to find the point where it touches the circle. From any point in the tangent line *a b*, as *e*, draw a line from the centre *e*; divide *e c*, into two equal parts at *d*; on *d* with the radius *d e*, or *d c*, describe an arch, cutting the given circle at *f*, which is the point required.

FIG. 6.

Through any three points given, to describe the circumference of a circle. Let *i d b*, be the given points; on *i d* and *b*, with any radius large enough to make the intersections *o e*, and *n c*, describe the arches *e o*, and *n c*; draw the lines *e a*, and *c a*, cutting *o*, and *n*, and meeting at *a*, the centre.

FIG. 7.

Two circles being given to make another circle to contain the same quantity. Let A and B be the two given circles; draw *a c*, cutting the two circles in their centres; on *c* erect a perpendicular; make *c d*, equal to *a b*, the diameter of the circle A; draw the line *d b*; divide *d b* into two equal parts at *e*; on *e*, with the distance *e d*, or *e b*, describe the circle D, which is equal, in size, to the two given circles A and B.

FIG. 8.

To draw a segment of a circle to any length and height. *a b*, is the length, *n c*, the height; divide the length *a b* into two equal parts by a perpendicular *f d*; divide *c b* by the same method, and their meeting at *f* will be the centre for drawing the arch *b c a*, which is the segment required.

FIG. 9.

To describe the representation of an ellipsis by centres. Divide *g h* into three equal parts at *d* and *r*; with that distance, and on *d* and *r*, make the intersections *i* and *o*; from *i*, through *d* and *r*, draw *i n*, and *i e*; from *o*, through *d* and *r*, draw *o c*, and *o a*; on *d* and *r*, describe the circles *c g e*, and *a h n*; on *o* and *i* describe the circles *a c*, and *n e*.

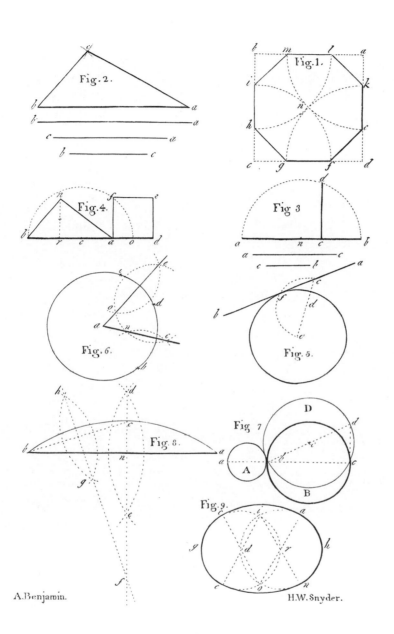

Fig. 2.

Fig. 1.

Fig. 4.

Fig 3

Fig. 6.

Fig. 5.

Fig 7

Fig. 8.

Fig. 9.

A. Benjamin.

H.W. Snyder.

PLATE IV.

FIG. 1.

To describe a representation of an ellipsis by centres. Divide *a b* into four equal parts ; with the distance *d d*, and on *d d*, describe the arches *e d c*, and *c d e* ; draw *c f, c i, e g*, and *e h* ; on *c* and *e*, with the distance *c f*, or *c i*, describe the arches *i f*, and *g h*, on *d*, and *d*, with the distance *d a*, or *d b*, describe the arches *f a g*, and *i b h*.

FIG. 2.

To make an ellipsis with a cord. Take half of the longer diameter *a c*, which is *a i*, or *c i* ; with that distance, fix one foot of the compasses in *o* ; intersect *a c* at *b* and *d* ; tack in a nail at *b* and *d*, then lay a cord round *d* and *b*, and make it meet at *o* ; fix a pencil at *o*, and move your hand around, keeping the cord tight, will describe an ellipsis.

FIG. 3.

To describe an ellipsis by ordinates. Make a circle with the radius *a c*, or *a b* ; divide the half circle into any number of parts, say 10 ; make *c* 5, perpendicular to *c b*, and equal to one half of the smaller diameter of the ellipsis ; draw ordinates through each of the ten divisions on the semicircle *c d b* ; draw *a* 5, then *c a* 5 will be the scale to set off your oval ; take 4, 1, from the scale, and set it from 1 to 1, in your oval both ways, and at each end ; then take 3, 2, from the scale, and set it from 2 to 2 each way on the oval ; find all the other points in the same manner ; a curve being traced through each of these points, will form the true ellipsis.

FIG. 4.

To describe an ellipsis by a trammel. *g f e*, is a trammel rod ; *g*, a nut, with a hole through it, to hold a pencil ; at *f* and *e*, are two other sliding nuts ; make the distance of *f*, from *g*, one half of the shorter diameter of the ellipsis, and from *g* to *e*, equal to one half of the longer diameter ; the points *f* and *e*, being put into grooves *d c*, and *a b*, then moving your pencil around at *g*, will describe a true curve of the ellipsis.

FIG. 5, *and* 6.

To draw a semiellipsis by the intersection of lines. Let the given axis be *a b*, and divide it into any number of parts, as 10 ; also let the height be divided into half that number of parts, as 5 ; make *e q* equal to *q k*, the height of the arch ; then from the point *e*, draw lines through the equal divisions of the axis *a b* ; likewise through the points, 1, 2, 3, 4, *c*, in the height *b c*, draw lines tending to the crown at *p*, which will intersect at the points, *o n m l*, and lines being drawn through the divisions of *a c*, at *p*, at the crown ; in the same manner will form the points *i h g f* ; a curve being traced through these points, will show the true curve of the ellipsis.

FIG. 7.

How to draw the segment of a circle by intersecting lines. Let *g e*, be the length of the segment, *a b*, its heigth ; draw the cord *b e*, and *b g* ; draw *e c*, and *g d*, at right angles with *b e*, and *b g*, and from the centre at *a*, divide *a e*, and *a g*, each into five equal parts ; also from *b*, at the crown, in the centre of the line *d c*, divide *b c*, and *b d*, each into five equal parts ; and draw 1 1, 2 2, 3 3, 4 4, *e c*, and *g d*, through the divisions 1, 2, 3, 4, 5, on *e* 5, and *g* 5, draw lines to the crown at *b*, which will intersect the other lines at the points *m n o r*, and *q f k i* ; the curve being traced, the segment will be complete.

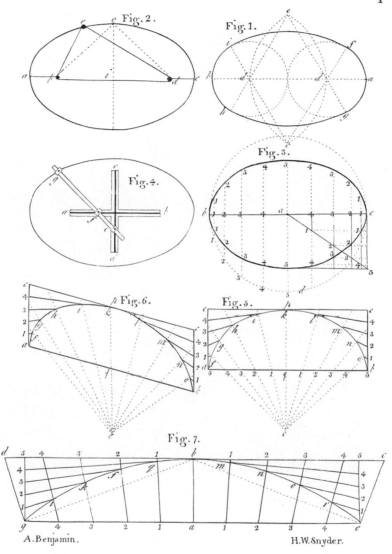

4

Fig. 2.

Fig. 1.

Fig. 4.

Fig. 3.

Fig. 6.

Fig. 5.

Fig. 7.

A. Benjamin.

H.W. Snyder.

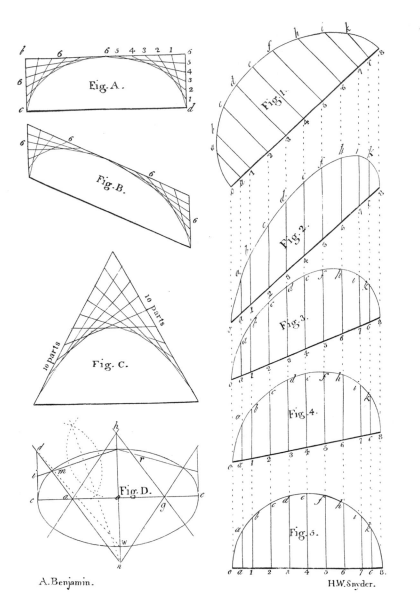

5

Fig. A.

Fig. B.

Fig. C.

10 parts

Fig. D.

Fig. 1.

Fig. 2.

Fig. 3.

Fig. 4.

Fig. 5.

A. Benjamin.

H.W. Snyder.

PLATE V.

FIG. A.

To describe a representation of a semiellipsis by the intersection of right lines. Let *c d* be the transverse diameter, *d* 6 equal to one half of the conjugate diameter ; divide *d* 6, and 6 6, each into six equal parts, and draw the lines *d* 1, 1 2, 2 3, 3 4, 4 5, and 5 6, which completes one half ; proceed in the same manner to draw the other half, and also to draw fig. B and C.

NOTE.—This way of representing an ellipsis is not a correct one ; but in most cases it will answer in practice, particularly, where exactness is not required. It may be observed, that the curve is changed by the number of parts you make use of ; if divided into a great number of parts, it makes the curve too quick ; if into a small number, it makes it too flat ; by taking the medium between these two extremes, you will approximate nigh the truth.

FIG. D.

The transverse and conjugate diameters of an ellipsis being given to draw its representation. Draw *c d* parallel, and equal to *o r*, bisect it in *i*, draw *i r*, and *d w*, cutting each other at *m*; bisect *m r*, by a perpendicular meeting *r w*, produced at *n*; draw *n d*, cutting *c e*, at *a*; make *o g*, equal to *o a*; *o h*, equal to *o n*, through the points *a*, *n*, *g*, *h*; draw the lines *n g*, *g h*, *h a*, and *n a*; and in the centres *n*, *g*, *h*, *a*, describe the four sectors, and it will produce the representation required.

FIG. 5.

Divide *o* 8 into any number of parts, and draw the ordinates, *a a*, 1 *b*, 2 *c*, 3 *d*, 4 *e*, 5 *f*, 6 *h*, 7 *i*, and *c k*; transfer those distances to *a a*, 1 *b*, 2 *c*, 3 *d*, 4 *e*, 5 *f*, &c. to figs. 4, 3, 2, and 1, and through the points, *o*, *a*, *b*, *c*, *d*, *e*, *f*, *h*, *i*, *k*, and 8, trace their curves and the thing is done.

PLATE VI.

FIG. 1.

How to find the curvature of the different ribs in plaister groins. Fig. I. A. Let *e n* 1 2 3 4 5 6 7 0 8, be the given arch, standing over *e n* 1 2 3 4, &c. to 8, on the plan, or any other position parallel to it ; let *e c*, and *a f*, be the angles of the plan over which the ribs are to be placed ; divide the base line *e* 8, of the given rib A, into any number of parts, and through those parts draw lines from the arch to the diagonal line *f c*, which is the base line of the rib D, continue them at right angles through the rib B, and transfer the distances in A, the given rib *n n*, 1 1, 2 2, 3 3, 4 4, 5 5, 6 6, 7 7, 0 0, to *n n*, 1 1, 2 2, 3 3, 4 4, 5 5, 6 6, 7 7, and 0 0, on D and B, and trace the curves, which will complete the angle rib D, and side rib D.

NOTE.   The ribs D and B, may be described with the trammel, which is laid down on plate 4, fig. 4.

FIG. 2.

To draw a segment of a circle by rods to any length and height.   Take two rods, *d h*, and *d a*, each equal to *o n*, the opening ; place them to the height at *d*, and to the end *o n*, put a piece across them *o c n*, to keep them tight, and move the rods around the points *o n*, and it will describe the segment at the point *d*.

FIG. 3.

How to find the raking mouldings for a pediment.   Let A, be the given moulding, B, the raking moulding, and D, the return moulding ; draw the line *e a*, in B, at right angles with the rake of the pediment, and *e a*, in D, perpendicular, or parallel to *e c*, in A ; make *c a* in B, and *c a* in D, each equal to *c a* in A ; divide the curve of the given cimarecta A, into any number of parts, as here, into four, and draw lines upon the rake and parallel to it ; with the distances 1 2, and 3 4, in A, make the points from 2 to 1, and 3 to 4, in B and D, and through those points trace the curves *e* 4, 1 n, in B, and *e* 4, 1 *c*, in D.

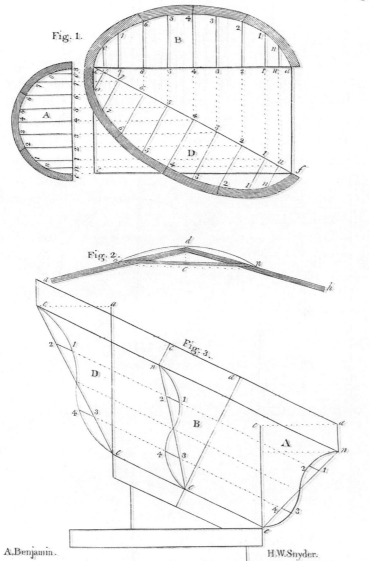

6

Fig. 1.

B

A

D

Fig. 2.

d

Fig. 3.

D

B

A

A.Benjamin.

H.W.Snyder.

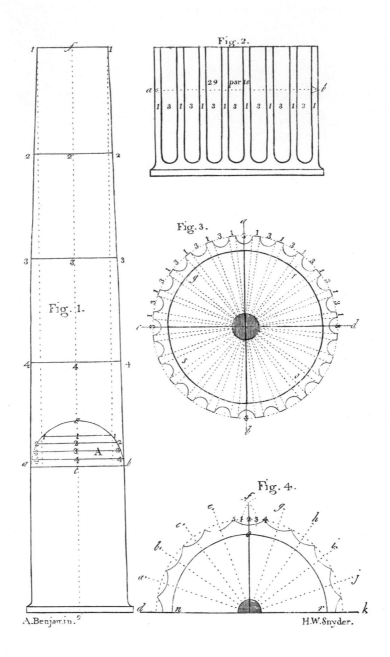

7

Fig. 2.

Fig. 1.

Fig. 3.

Fig. 4.

A. Benjamin.

H.W. Snyder.

PLATE VII.

FIG. 1.

How to diminish the shaft of a column.   Let 6 f, be the central line ; divide it into four parts, and at one fourth make the line a b across the column ; on c, make the half circle a e b ; with the distance f 1, at the neck of the column, and on 1, on the central line, make the points 1, 1, on the circle ; divide from 1 to c, into four parts ; also, from c to f into four parts, and draw lines through each of those divisions ; and with the distances 2 2, 3 3, and 4 4 in A, on the line 6 f, make the points 2 2, 3 3, 4 4, on the sides of the column, and in those points, and in 1 b, and 1 a, tack in nails or brads, bend a lath around them, and by it mark the curves.

FIG. 2.

How to set out flutes and fillets on a pilaster.   Divide a b into twenty nine equal parts, and give three of them to each flute, and one to a fillet.

FIG. 3.

How to set out flutes and fillets of a column.   Draw the lines a b, and c d, through the centre of the column, and at right angles with each other ; divide the circumference of the column into ninety six equal parts ; with one and one half of those parts in your compasses, and on the lines a b, and c d, at 3, 3, 3, 3, describe the flutes ; the circle r o s g, is the size of the column at its neck, where the flutes and fillets are divided, by drawing each line of the fillets across it, pointing to the centre.

FIG. 4.

Shows how to set out flutes, without fillets, on the Doric column.   Divide the circumference into twenty equal parts ; with three fourths of one of those parts, on the points 5 and 4, make the intersection f, and on f, describe the flute 5 4 ; d a b c e g h i j and k, are also centres for drawing the other flutes ; n o r, is the size of the column at its neck.

PLATE VIII.

FIG. 1.

To draw the Ionic volute. Draw a geometrical square within the eye of the volute, and bisect its sides in the points 1 3, and 2 4; and from those points, draw the lines 1 3, and 2 4; divide each of them into six equal parts; see A, the eye, at large; place one foot of the compasses at 1, on the side of the geometrical square, and extend the other to *d*, and draw the arch *d e*; then with the distance 2 *e*, and on 2, describe the arch *e f*; on 3, and with the distance *3 f*, describe the arch *f g*; with the distance 4 *g*, and on 4, describe the arch *g i*; and with the distance 5 *i*, and on 5, describe *i k*; and with the distance 6 *k*, describe *k n*; and with the distance 7 *n*, describe *n o*; and with the distance 8 *o*, describe *o m*; and with the distance 9 *m*, describe *m r*; with 10 *r*, describe *r s*; with 11 *s*, describe *s t*; with 12 *t*, describe *t u*; and on *n*, describe *d a*, which completes the outside line.

To describe the inside line, which diminishes the fillet, divide 1 5 in A, into five equal parts, and set one of them from 1 2 3 4 5 6 7 8 9 10 11 and 12, toward the centre of the eye, which will be the twelve centres for drawing the inside line.

FIG. 2.

To draw the representation of an elliptical volute. Draw the line *b a*, cutting the eye in its centre; divide 2 *g*, the diameter of the eye, into six equal parts; on *g*, with the distance *g a*, describe a half circle *a b*; on 2, and with the distance 2 *b*, describe the circle *b c*; on 3, and with the distance 3 *c*, describe *c d*; on 4, and with the distance 4 *d*, describe *d e*; on 5, and with the distance 5 *e*, describe *e f*; on 6, and with the distance 6 *f*, describe *f g*; to draw the inside line, divide one sixth of the diameter of the eye into five parts, and set one of them from *g* 2 3 4 5 and 6, toward the centre of the eye, which will be the centres for drawing the inside line. B, is the eye at large.

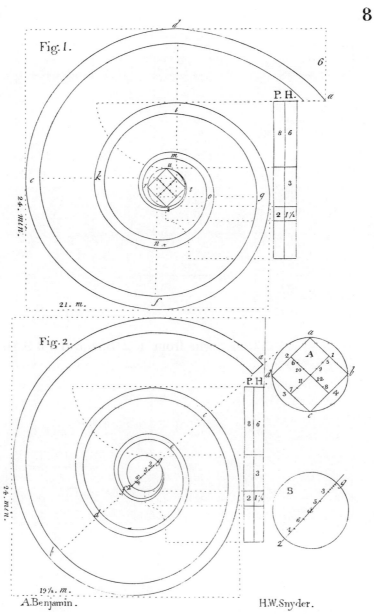

Fig. 1.

P. H.

24. m.m.

21. m.

Fig. 2.

P. H.

A

B

24. m.m.

19½. m.

A. Benjamin.   H. W. Snyder.

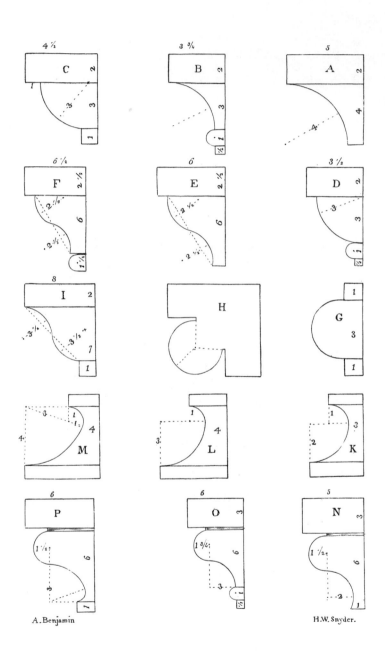

A.Benjamin   H.W.Snyder.

PLATES IX AND X.

On plate 9, are fifteen, and on the lower part of plate 10, are six designs for mouldings, all of which have their particular parts figured; and the centres for drawing their curves, are marked on the plates, which, I think, will make them sufficiently plain, without any further explanation.

PLATE X.

To describe the quirk ovolo, A.   With one fourth of $i\,k$, in your compasses, and on d, which is two and one half parts from the line $i\,k$, describe the arch $n\,e$, with the distance $a\,b$; from a and e, make the point of intersection at c; on c, describe the arch $a\,e$, which completes the moulding.

The above directions will be observed in describing B and C; the only difference in them is, their projections; A, projects four parts, B, five parts, and C, six parts.

To draw the quirk ovolo D, and the hollow E.   Draw the lines $a\,b$ in D and E, and divide $a\,b$ in F, into eight parts; draw lines from each of those parts, at right angles with $a\,b$ in F, and parallel to the fillets of D and E, cutting the lines $a\,b$ in D and E, at 2 4 9 7 10 12 and 14; transfer the distances 1 2, 3 4, 5 9, 6 7, 8 10, 11 12, 13 14, in F, to 1 2, 3 4, 5 9, 6 7, 8 10, 11 12, 13 14, in D and E, and by those points trace their curves and they are complete.   In the same way may those mouldings be drawn to any projection.

PLATE IX.

NAMES OF MOULDINGS.

A, cavetto, or hollow; B, cavetto and astrigal; C, ovolo and fillet; D, ovolo and astrigal; E, cimareversa, or ogee; F, cimareversa and bead; G, astrigal; H, bead; I, cimarecta; K, L, and M, are scoties of different projections and curves; N, O, P, are quirk ogees.

NOTE.—If mouldings are only composed of parts of a circle, and straight lines, they are called Roman; because the Romans, in their buildings, seldom or never, employed any other curve for mouldings, than that of a circle; but if a moulding, is made of part of an ellipsis, or a parabola, or any hyperbole, the mouldings are then in the Grecian taste; hence it appears, that mouldings of the Grecian taste, are of much greater variety than those of the Roman, where only parts of circles are concerned.

Although I have made use of the Roman ovolo and ogee in all the orders, I do not generally use them in practice; the bending, or turning inward, of the upper edge of the Grecian, or quirk ovolo, when the sun shines on its surface, causes a beautiful variety of light and shade, which greatly relieves it from plane surfaces; and if it is entirely in shadow, but receive a reflected light, the bending, or turning inward, at the top, will cause it to contain a greater quantity of shade in that place, but softened downward around the moulding to the under edge. In the Roman ovolo there is no turning inward, at the top; therefore, when the sun shines on its surface, it will not be so bright, on its upper edge, as the Grecian ovolo; nor will it cause so beautiful a line of distinction from the other mouldings, with which it is combined, when it is in shadow, and when lighted by reflection.

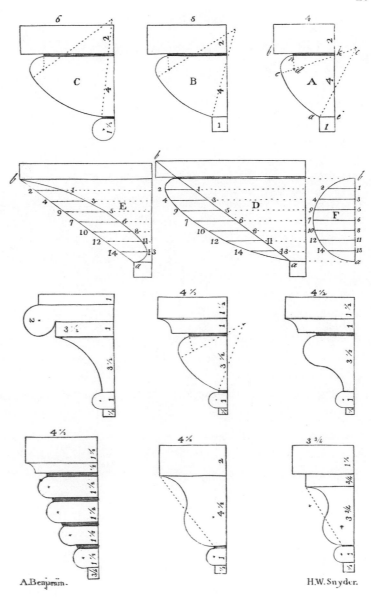

10

A. Benjamin.   H.W. Snyder.

In the Greek ogee, the turning in of its upper edge, and the turning out of its under edge, will, when the sun shines bright, cause it to be very bright on these edges, which will greatly relieve it from other perpendicular surfaces when combined together ; and when it is in shadow, and lighted by reflection, the inclination of the upper and under edges will also make a strong line of distinction, on both edges, between it and other mouldings, or, of planes connected with it ; whereas the upper and under edges of the Roman ogee, being perpendicular to the horizon, the lightest place on its surface will not be lighter than a perpendicular plane surface ; nor will it be better relieved in shadow than perpendicular plane surfaces, also in shadow.

PLATE XI.

FIG. 1.

To describe the Grecian ovolo, the tangent *a b*, at the bottom, and the point of contact *a*, and the greatest projection of the moulding at *c*, being given. From *a*, draw *a d e*, perpendicular; through *c*, draw *c b* parallel to it; also, through *c*, draw *c d* parallel to the tangent *b a*, cutting *a e* at *d*; make *d e* equal to *a d*, then will *d* be the centre of an ellipsis, and *c d* and *d a*, will be two semiconjugate diameters, from which the ellipsis may be described; divide *b c* and *c d*, each into a like number of equal parts; from the point *a*, and through the points 1, 2, 3, in *b c*, draw lines; also from *e*, through the points 1, 2, 3, in *c d*, draw lines cutting the former at 4, 5, 6, which will give the points through which the curve is to be traced.

FIG. 2.

This figure is described in the same manner as fig. 1. It has a greater projection, the tangent being also taken in a higher position.

FIG. 3.

To describe a scotia. Join the ends of each fillet by the right line *a b*; bisect *a b* at *d*; through *d*, draw *c d e* parallel to the fillets, and make *c d*, and *d e*, each equal to the depth of the scotia; divide *d a*, *d b*, *b f*, and *a g*, each into a like number of equal parts; from the point *e*, and through the points 1, 2, 3, in *a g* and *b f*, draw lines; also from *c*, through the points 1, 2, 3, in *d a* and *d b*, draw lines, cutting the former at the points 4, 5, 6, and 7, 8, 9, through which points the curve is to be traced.

FIG. 4, 5, *and* 6.

Draw *g f*, a continuation of the upper side of the under fillet; through *b*, draw *b g*, perpendicular to *g f*, cutting it at *g*, and the tangent *f c*, at the point *c*; also

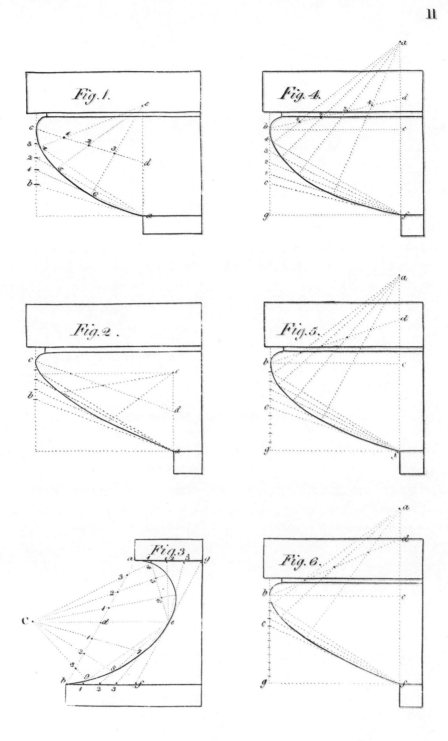

Fig.1.

Fig.2.

Fig.3.

Fig.4.

Fig.5.

Fig.6.

through *b*, draw *b e* parallel to *g f*, and through *f*, draw *f e d a*, parallel to *g b*, cutting *b e* at *e ;* make *e a* equal to *e f ; e d* equal to *c g*, and join *b d ;* then divide each of the lines *b c* and *b d*, into a like number of equal parts ; from the point *f*, and through the points 1, 2, 3, 4, in *b c*, draw lines ; also from *a*, through the points 1, 2, 3, 4, in *b d*, draw lines, cutting the former, which will give the points required, by which to trace the curves.

N. B. By these means you may make a moulding to any form you please, whether flat or round. The difference produced in the curves of figs. 5, and 6, from that of 4, is occasioned by the tangent line *f c*, cutting *g b*, nearer to *b*, in figs. 5, and 6, than in fig. 4.

THE ORIGIN OF BUILDING.

BUILDINGS were certainly among the first wants of mankind; and architecture must, undoubtedly, be classed among the earliest antediluvian arts. Scripture informs us that Cain built a city; and soon after the deluge we hear of many cities, and of an attempt to build a tower that should reach the sky. A miracle stopped the progress, and prevented the completion of that bold design.

The first men, living in a warm climate, wanted no habitations; every grove afforded a shade from the rays of the sun, and shelter from the dews of the night; rain fell but seldom, nor was it ever sufficiently cold to render closer dwellings than groves, either desirable or necessary, even in the hours of repose. They fed upon the spontaneous productions of the soil, and lived without care, and without labour.

But when the human species increased, and the produce of the earth, however luxuriant, was insufficient to supply the requisite food. When frequent disappointments drew on contention, with all its train of calamities, then separation became necessary, and colonies dispersed to different regions, where frequent rains, storms, and piercing cold, forced the inhabitants to seek for better shelter than trees.

At first they most likely retired to caverns, formed by nature in rocks, to hollow trunks of trees, or to holes dug by themselves in the earth; but soon disgusted with the damp and darkness of these habitations, they began to search after more wholesome and comfortable dwellings.

The animal creation pointed out both materials and manners of construction. Swallows, rooks, bees, and storks, were the first builders. Man observed their instinctive operations; he admired; he imitated; and being endued with reasoning faculties, and of a structure suited to mechanical purposes, he soon outdid his masters in the builder's art.

Rude and unseemly, doubtless, were the first attempts; without experience or tools the builder collected a few bows of trees, spread them in a conic shape, and covering them with rushes or leaves and clay, formed his hut; sufficient to shelter its hardy inhabitants at night, or in seasons of bad weather. But in the course of time man naturally grew more expert; they invented tools to shorten and improve labour; fell upon neater, more durable modes of construction; and forms better adapted than the cone, to the purposes for which their huts were intended. They felt the want of convenient habitations, wherein to taste the comforts of privacy, to rest securely, and be effectually screened from troublesome excesses of weathers. They wanted room to exercise the arts, to which necessity had given birth; to deposit the grain that agriculture enabled them to raise in abundance; to secure the flocks which frequent disappointments in the chace, forced them to collect and domesticate. Thus stimulated, their fancy and hands went arduously to work, and the progress of improvement was rapid.

That the primitive hut was of a conic figure it is reasonable to conjecture; for of that form do the American Aborigines build their wigwams; and from its being simplest of the solid forms, and most easily constructed. And wherever wood was found, they probably built in the manner above described; but, soon as the inhabitants discovered the inclined sides, and the want of upright space in the cone, they changed it for the cube; and as it is supposed, proceeded in the following manner.

Having, says Vitruvius, marked out the space to be occupied by the hut, they fixed in the ground several upright trunks of trees to form the sides, filling the intervals between them with branches, closely interwoven, and spread over with clay. The sides thus completed, four beams were laid on the upright trunks, which, being well fastened together at the angles of their junction, kept the sides firm; and likewise served to support the covering, or roof of the building, composed of smaller trees, placed horizontally like joists, upon which, were laid several beds of reeds, leaves, and earth, or clay.

By degrees, other improvements took place; and means were found to make the fabric lasting, neat and handsome, as well as convenient. The bark and other protuberances were taken from the trees that formed the sides; these trees were raised above the dirt and humidity, on stones; were covered at the top with other stones and firmly bound round at both ends with ozier, or cords, to secure them from splitting. The spaces between the joists of the roof, were closed up with clay or wax, and the ends of them either smoothed, or covered with boards.

The different beds of materials that composed the covering, were cut straight at the eaves, and distinguished from each other by different projections. The form of the roof too was altered ; for being, on account of its flatness, unfit to throw off the rains which sometimes fell in great abundance, it was raised in the middle, on trees disposed like rafters, after the form of a gable roof.

This construction, simple as it appears, probably gave birth to most of the parts that now adorn our buildings ; particularly to the orders, which may be considered as the basis of the whole decorative part of architecture ; for when structures of wood were set aside, and men began to erect solid, stately edifices of stone, having nothing nearer to imitate, they naturally copied the parts which necessity introduced in the primitive hut ; insomuch that the upright trees, with the stones and cordage at each end of them, were the origin of columns, bases, and capitals ; the beams and joists, gave rise to architraves and friezes, with their triglyphs and metops ; and the gable roof was the origin of pediments ; as the beds of materials, forming the covering, and the rafters supporting them, were of cornices ; with their corona, their mutules, modillions, and dentils.

As, in many other arts, so in architecture, there are certain elementary forms, which, though simple in their nature, and few in number, are the principal constituent objects of every composition, however complicated or extensive it may be.

OF THE PARTS WHICH COMPOSE THE ORDERS OF ARCHITECTURE, AND OF THEIR PROPERTIES, APPLICATION, AND EMBELLISHMENTS.

Of these there are, in this art, two distinct sorts ; the first consisting of such parts, as represent those that were essentially necessary in the construction of the primitive huts ; as the shaft of the column, with the plinth of its base, and the abacus of its capital, representing the upright trees, with the stones used to raise, and to cover them. Likewise the architrave and triglyph, representing the beams and joists ; the mutules, modillions, and dentils, either representing the rafters, or some other pieces of timber employed to support the covering ; and the corona, representing the beds of materials which composed the covering itself. All these are properly distinguished by the appellation of essential parts, and form the first class. The subservient members, contrived for the use and ornament of these, and intended either to support, to shelter, or to unite them gracefully together, which are usually called mouldings, constitute the second class.

Of regular mouldings, there are eight, which are, the fillet, the astragal or bead, the cimareversa or ogee, the cimarecta, the cavetto or hollow, the ovolo or quarter round, the scotia, and the torus.

The names of these are allusive to their forms; and the forms are adapted to the uses which they are intended to serve. The ovolo and ogee, being strong at their extremities are fit for supports; the cimarecta and cavetto, though improper for that purpose, as they are weak in the extreme parts, and terminate in a point, are well contrived for coverings to shelter other members; the tendency of their outline being very opposite to the direction of falling water, which, for that reason, cannot glide along their surface, but must necessarily drop. The torus and astragal, shaped like ropes, are intended to bind and strengthen the parts on which they are employed; and the use of the fillet and scotia, is only to separate, contrast, and strengthen the effect of the other mouldings; to give a graceful turn to the profile, and to prevent that confusion, which would be occasioned by joining several convex members together.

An assemblage of essential parts and mouldings, is termed a profile; and on the choice, dispositions, and proportions of these, depend the beauty or deformity of the composition. The most perfect profiles, are such as consist of few mouldings, varied both in form and size; fitly applied, with regard to their uses, and so distributed, that the straight and curved ones, succeed each other alternately. In every profile, there should be a predominant member, to which all the others ought to seem subservient; and made, either to support, to fortify, or to shelter it from injuries of weather; and whenever the profile is considerable, or much complicated, the predominant should always be accompanied with one, or more, other principal members; in form and dimension, calculated to attract the eye; create momentary pauses; and assist the perception of the beholder. These predominant and principal members, ought always to be of the essential class, and generally rectangular. Thus, in a cornice, the corona predominate; the modillions and dentiles are principals in the compositions; the cimarecta and cavetto, cover them; the ovolo and ogee, support them.

When ornaments are employed to decorate a profile, some of the mouldings should always be left plain, in order to form a proper repose ; for when all are enriched, the figure of the profile is lost in confusion.   In an entablature, the corona should not be ornamented ; nor the modillion band ; neither should the plinths of column, fillets, nor scarcely any square members be carved ; for, generally speaking, they are either principal in the composition, or used as boundaries to other parts : in both which cases their figures should be simple, distinct and unembarrassed.   The dentil band should remain uncut, where the ovolo and ogee immediately above and below it are enriched ; for when the dentils are marked, the three members are confounded together and being covered with ornaments, become far too rich for the remainder of the composition, which are defects, at all times studiously to be avoided ; as a distinct outline, and an equal distribution of enrichments, must, on every occasion, be strictly attended to.

Ornaments should neither be too frugally employed, nor distributed with too much profusion ; their value will increase, in proportion to the judgment and discretion shown in their application.

Variety in ornaments should not be carried to an excess.   In architecture they are only accessaries ; and therefore they should not be too striking, nor capable of long detaining the attention from the main object. Those of the mouldings in particular, should be simple, uniform, and never composed of more than two different representations upon each moulding ; which ought to be cut each equally deep ; be formed of the same number of parts ; all nearly of the same dimensions, in order to produce one even uninterrupted hue throughout ; that so the eye may not be more strongly attracted by any part in particular, than by the whole composition.

All the ornaments in the entablature are to be governed by the modillions, or mutules ; and the distribution of these must depend on the intervals of the columns ; and be so disposed, that one of them may come directly over the axis of each column.   It is farther to be observed, that the ornaments must partake of the character of the order they enrich ; those used in the Doric and Ionic orders, are to be of simple forms, and of larger bulk than those employed in the Corinthian or Composite.

When friezes, or other larger members, are to be enriched, the ornaments may be significant, and serve to indicate the destination, or use of the building; the rank, qualities, profession, and achievments of the owner.

In sacred places, all obscene, grotesque, and heathenish representations ought to be avoided; for indecent fables, extravagant conceits, or instruments and symbols of pagan worship, are very improper ornaments in structures consecrated to christian devotion.

With regard to the manner of executing ornaments, it is to be remembered, that, as in sculpture, drapery is not estimable, unless its folds are contrived to grace, and indicate the parts and articulations of the body it covers; so in architecture, the most exquisite ornaments lose all their value, if they load, alter, or confuse the form they are designed to enrich and adorn.

The method of the ancient sculptors, in the execution of architectonic ornaments, was, to aim at a perfect representation of the object they chose to imitate; so that the chesnuts, acorns, or eggs, with which the ovolo is commonly enriched, are, in the antiques, cut round, and almost entirely detached; as are likewise the berries, or beads, on the astragal, which are generally as much hollowed into the solid of the body, as the moulding projects beyond it; but the leaves, shells, and flowers, that adorn the cavetto, cima, ogee, and torus, are kept flat, like the things they represent.

In the application of their ornaments, they observed to use such as required a considerable relief on mouldings, that in themselves are clumsy, as the ovolo and astragal; which, by means of the deep incisions made in them to form these enrichments, acquired an extraordinary lightness; but on more elegant parts, as the cavetto, and cima, they employed thin bodies, which could be represented without entering too far into the solid. The ornaments of their cornices were boldly marked, that they might be distinguished from afar; but those of the basis of columns, or of pedestals, being nearer the eye, were more slightly expressed; as well on that account, as because it would have been improper to weaken these parts, and impossible to keep them clean, had there been any deep cavities in them, to harbour dust or filth.

When objects are near, and liable to close inspection, every part of the orna-ment should be expressed, and well finished ; but when they are much exalted, the detail may be slightly touched, or entirely neglected ; for it is sufficient if the general form be distinct, and the principal masses strongly marked. A few rough strokes from the hand of a skilful master, are much more effectual than the most elaborate finishings of an artless imitator; which, seldom consisting in more than smoothing and neatly rounding off the parts, are calculated to destroy, rather than to produce effect.

OF THE ORDERS OF ARCHITECTURE IN GENERAL.

THE orders of architecture, as has been observed, are the basis upon which the whole decorative part of the art is chiefly built, and toward which the atten-tion of the artist must ever be directed, even where no orders are introduced. In them, originate most of the forms used in decoration ; they regulate most of the proportions ; and to their combination, multiplied, varied, and arranged, in a thousand different ways, architecture is indebted for its most splendid pro-ductions.

These orders are different modes of building, said, originally, to have been imitated from the primitive huts ; being composed of such parts as were essen-tial in their construction, and afterward also in the temples of antiquity ; which, though at first simple and rude, were, in the course of time, and by the ingenuity of succeeding architects, wrought up and improved, to such a pitch of perfec-tion, that they were by way of excellence, distinguished by the name of orders.

Of these there are five ; three said to be of Grecian origin, are called Grecian orders ; being distinguished by the names of Doric, Ionic, and Corinthian ; they exhibit three distinct characters of composition ; supposed to have been suggested by the diversity of character in the human frame. The remaining two, being of Italian origin, are called Latin orders ; they are distinguished by the names of Tuscan and Roman, and were probably invented with a view of extending the characteristic bounds, on one side, still farther toward strength and similarity ; as on the other toward elegance and profusion of enrichments.

At what time the orders were invented, or by whom improved to the utmost, remains, at least, doubtful. And of their origin little is known but from the relation of Vitruvius ; the veracity of which has been much questioned, and is, probably, not much to be depended on.

" Dorus," says he, " son of Helenes and the nymph Optica, king of Achaia and of all the Peloponnesus, having formerly built a temple to Juno, in the ancient city of Argos ; this temple happened to be in the manner which is called Doric ; and was afterward imitated in many others, built in the several cities of Achaia.

" About the same time, the Athenians, after having consulted the oracle of Apollo, at Delphos, by the common consent of all Greece, sent into Asia thirteen colonies, each under the command of a separate captain ; but all under the general direction of Ion, son of Xuthus and Creusa. Ion being arrived in Asia, conquered all Caria, and founded thirteen large cities ; the inhabitants whereof, having expelled the Carians and Leleges, called the country Ionia, in honor of Ion, their leader ; and erected temples, of which the first, dedicated to Apollo Panionius, was built after the manner of those they had seen in Achaia, which they called Doric, because temples of the same sort had been erected in the cities of the Dorians.

" But some time after, building a temple to Diana, different from these, and of a more delicate structure ; being formed upon the proportions of a female body, as the Doric had been on those of a robust man ; and adorning the capitals of their columns with volutes, to represent the curls of a woman's hair ; and the shafts with flutings, to express the folds of her garment. They gave to this second manner of building the name of Ionic ; because it was invented, and first used by the Ionians.

" The third sort of columns, which are called Corinthian, and represent the delicate figure of a young girl, owe their birth to the following accident.

" A young woman of Corinth being dead, her nurse placed on her tomb a basket, containing certain trinkets, in which she delighted, when alive ; covering it with a tile to shelter them from the weather. The basket happened accidentally to be set on a root of the acanthus, which pushing forth its leaves and sprigs in the spring, covered the sides of it ; and some of them, longer than the rest, being obstructed by the angles of the tile, were forced downward, and by degrees, curled into the form of volutes.

" Callimachus, a celebrated sculptor, passing near the tomb, observed the basket and in how graceful a manner the leaves of the acanthus had surrounded it ; the form pleased him exceedingly ; he imitated it on the tops of some columns, which he afterward executed at Corinth ; establishing and regulating by this model, the manner and proportions of the Corinthian order."

Of the two Latin orders, the Tuscan is said to have been invented by the inhabitants of Tuscany, before the Romans had intercourse with the Greeks, or were acquainted with their arts ; whence it is called Tuscan. Probably, however, these people, originally a colony of Greeks, only imitated, in the best manner they could, what they remembered in their own country ; simplifying the Doric, either to expedite their work, or perhaps, to adapt it to the abilities of their workmen.

The second Latin order, though of Roman production, is but of modern adoption ; the ancients never having considered it as a distinct order. It is a mixture of the Ionic and Corinthian ; and is now distinguished by the names of Roman, or Composite.

The ingenuity of man has, hitherto, not been able to produce a sixth order, though large premiums have been offered, and numerous attempts made, by men of the first rate talents to accomplish it. Such is the fettered human imagination ; such the scanty store of its ideas, that Doric, Ionic, and Corinthian, have ever floated uppermost ; and all that has ever been produced, amounts to nothing more than different arrangements and combinations of their parts.

An order is composed of two principal members ; the column, and the entablature ; each of which is divided into three principal parts. Those of the column, are the base, the shaft, and the capital. Those of the entablature, are the architrave, the frieze, and the cornice. All these are again subdivided into many smaller parts ; the disposition, number, forms, and dimensions, of which, characterize each order, and express the degree of strength or delicacy, richness or simplicity peculiar to it.

The simplest, and most solid of all, is the Tuscan. It is composed of few, and large parts, devoid of ornaments ; and is of a construction so massive, that it seems capable of supporting the heaviest burdens.

There is no regular example of this order among the remains of antiquity. Piranisi has given a drawing of a Tuscan base, found at Rome, but of what date is uncertain. Vitruvius, in an indistinct manner, has mentioned its general proportions ; but through his whole book does not refer to one structure of this order. The Trajan and Antonine columns at Rome are reckoned of the Tuscan order ; they have eight diameters for their height : the torus and capitals are certainly more ornamented than is consistent with Tuscan plainness. The fluting to the necks also are after the most ancient Doric examples. It is somewhat singular there should be no remains of this order ; and were it not for what little Vitruvius has written of it, it certainly might have been lost to the moderns. The plainness of its appearance, no doubt, caused it to be neglected at Rome ; but in no other place has been discovered any truly ancient example.

As this order conveys ideas of strength and rustic simplicity, it may very properly be used for rural purposes ; for farm-houses, barns, sheds, stables, and greenhouses ; for gates of parks and gardens ; for prisons, arsenals ; also, in colonades and porticos, surrounding squares, markets, and granaries, or storehouses ; and generally, wherever magnificence is not required, and expense is to be avoided.

The design, here annexed, and also the Doric, Ionic, Corinthian, and Composite orders, I have selected from several authors, and have made all the alterations, that in my opinion, were necessary to render them conformable to the practice of the present time.

The Doric order, next in strength to the Tuscan, and of a grave, robust, masculine aspect, is, by Scammozzi, called the Herculean. Being the most ancient of all the orders, it retains more of the structure of the primitive huts, in its form, than any of the rest ; having triglyphs in the frieze, to represent the ends of joists ; and mutules in its cornice, to represent rafters, with inclined soffits, to express their direction in the originals, from whence they were imitated. Its column too, is often seen in ancient works, executed without a base, in imitation of the trees, used in the first buildings, without any plinths to raise them above the ground. Delicate ornaments are repugnant to its characteristic solidity, and it succeeds best, in the simple regularity of its proportions. Nosegays and garlands of flowers grace not a Hercules, who always appears more becomingly, with a rough club and lion's skin. For there are beauties of various sorts, and often so dissimilar, in their natures, that those which may be highly proper on one occasion, may be quite the reverse, even ridiculously absurd, on others.

The ancients employed the Doric in temples dedicated to Minerva, to Mars, and to Hercules; whose grave and manly dispositions, suited well with the character of this order. Serlio, says it is proper for churches dedicated to Jesus Christ; to St. Paul, St. Peter, or any other saints, remarkable for their fortitude, in exposing their lives, and suffering for the christian faith. It may be employed in the houses of generals, or other martial men; in mausoleums erected to their memory; likewise in all kinds of military buildings; as arsenals, gates of fortified places, guard-rooms, and similar structures.

The Ionic, being the second of the Grecian orders, holds a middle station, between the other two; and stands in equipoise between the grave solidity of the Doric, and the elegant delicacy of the Corinthian. Among the antiques, however, we find it in different dresses; sometimes more simple, and bordering on Doric plainness, all according to the fancy of the architect, or nature of the structure where employed. It is, throughout, of a more slender construction than either of the afore described orders; its appearance, though simple, is graceful and majestic; its ornaments should be few; rather neat than luxuriant.

As the Doric order is, particularly in churches or temples, dedicated to male saints, so the Ionic is principally used in such as are consecrated to females of the matronal state. It is likewise employed in courts of justice, in libraries, colleges, seminaries, and other structures, having relation to arts or letters; and in private houses; and in all places dedicated to peace and tranquillity. The ancients employed it in temples sacred to Juno, to Bacchus, to Diana, and other deities, whose dispositions held a medium between the severe and the effeminate.

The Corinthian.   Its proportions are elegant in the extreme ; every part of the order is divided into a great variety of members ; and abundantly enriched with a diversity of ornaments.   The ancients, says De Chambray, aiming at the representation of a feminine beauty, omitting nothing, either calculated to embellish, or capable of perfecting their work.   And he observes, that in many examples left of this order, such a profusion of different ornaments is introduced, that they seem to have exhausted imagination in the contrivance of decorations for this masterpiece of the art.

The ancients frequently employed the Ionic entablature in the Corinthian order, as appears by many of the buildings ; and sometimes, according to Vitruvius, even the Doric.

When the modillion cornice is employed on large concave surfaces, the sides of the modillions and coffers of the soffit, should tend toward the centre of the curve ; but when the concave is small, it will be better to direct them toward the opposite point in the circumference, that the contraction may be less perceptible, and the parts dependant thereon, suffer less deviation from the natural form.   The same rules must be observed with regard to dentils, to the abacus and bases of columns or pilasters, and likewise to the flanks of the pilaster itself. But on a convex surface, the sides of these should be parallel to each other ; for it would be unnatural and very disagreeable, to see them the narrowest where they spring out of the cornice, diverging as they advance forward, forming sharp angles, and a sort of mutilated triangular plan, with enlarged solids, and diminished intervals ; all calculated to destroy the usual proportions and beauty of the composition.

The Corinthian order is proper for all buildings, where elegance, gaiety and magnificence are required.   The ancients employed it in temples dedicated to Venus, to Flora, Proserpine, and the nymphs of fountains ; because the flowers, foliage, and volutes, with which it is adorned, seemed well adapted to the delicacy and elegance of such deities.   Being the most splendid of all the orders, it is proper for the decoration of squares, or galleries and arcades, surrounding them ; for churches, and on account of its rich, gay, and graceful appearance, it may with propriety, be used in theatres, in ball or banqueting rooms, and in all places consecrated to festive mirth, or convivial recreation.

Care must be taken in Corinthian, as well as in Composite capitals, that the feet of the lower leaves, do not project beyond the upper part of the shaft of the column ; because they then hide a considerable part of the upper row of leaves, and give a stunted, disagreeable form to the whole capital.   The different divisions of the acanthus leaf, and bunches of olive or parsely, which compose the total of each leaf, must be firmly marked, and massed in a very distinct manner ; the stems that spring from between the upper leaves, are to be kept low upon the vase of the capital, while rising between the leaves, then spring gradually forward, to form the different volutes.

The Composite or Roman order, certainly owes its origin to that constant solicitude after novelty, which ever renders the mind of man restless in an enlightened and highly cultivated age.   The desire of variety and novelty, either of new invention, or combination, certainly engaged the Roman architects to unite with the proportions and enrichments of the Corinthian order, the angular volute, and dentils of the Ionic, and by this union to compose a new order.

The introduction of the angular Ionic volute, and the omission of the upper row of leaves in the capital, certainly give it a more bold and noble aspect, than that of the Corinthian capital, yet different from any of the other orders, possessing an elegance and projection very pleasing, and may be used with very agreeable and happy effects.

There are many examples remaining at Rome, which show the general esti- mation of this order there, in the height of its splendour and prosperity. In their triumphal arches it was used with good effect, where it produced an agreeable boldness, uniting elegance and ornament.

The example here given of the column, its base, and capital, is that executed in the triumphal arch, erected in honor of Vespasian and Titus at Rome.

The entablature is nearly a copy of that of Sir William Chambers.

The cornice differs from the Corinthian, only in the modillions, which are square, and composed of two facias.   The soffit of the intervals between the dentils, may be hollowed upward behind the little fillet in front, which occasions a dark shade, that marks the dentil more distinctly.   And the same method may be observed in the Ionic and Corinthian orders, for the same reason.   The roses in the soffit of the corona, are not to project beyond its horizontal surface.

The Romans used the Composite order more frequently in the ir triumphal arches, than in any other buildings ; meaning to express their dominion over those nations, that invented the orders of which this is composed.   It may, with propriety, be used, wherever elegance and magnificence are to be united ; but it is more particularly adapted to buildings, designed to commemorate signal events, or, to celebrate the virtues and achievments of conquerors and legislators ; because the capitals, and other ornaments, may be composed of emblems, and of allusive representations.

PLATE XII.

To draw the Tuscan order to any given height. Divide E F, fig. B, into thirty nine equal parts ; take four of them for the diameter of the column, just above its base, as the scale i, k, which is divided into sixty equal parts, and are called minutes ; first divide $i\ k$ into twelve equal parts, then one twelfth, as $5\ k$, into five, each of which is called a minute ;* then each member of the order is so many minutes of this scale, either in height or projection.

If it should be necessary to add a subplinth, divide the whole height into forty-three equal parts ; give four of them to the diameter of the column, and four, or one diameter to the height of the subplinth ; if a pedestal be required, divide the whole height into forty-eight parts ; take four of them for the diameter of the column, and give nine, or two diameters and fifteen minutes to the height of the pedestal. On plate 21 is a block cornice, which may sometimes be used instead of the plain one, where it is seen at a considerable distance ; draw it by the same scale by which the rest of the order is drawn.

To diminish the column, divide its shaft into three equal parts ; leave the lowest third part undiminished ; divide the remaining two thirds into any number of parts, as three at 1, 2, and 50, and divide the difference of the semidiameter $e\ i$ in B, or $b\ a$, on A, at the top, into three equal parts ; draw a line from C, at the base of A, to 2 at the top, which will intersect the line 2, 3, at 3 ; then draw a line from C to 1, which will intersect 1, 4, at 4, tack in brads at C, 4, 3, and a ; bend a thin lath or strip, round them, and you will have the contour or curve of the column.

Note. Figs. A, and B, are diminishing rules ; I have explained that of A, which shows the same thing as B, which is not in its just proportion, but clearer to inspection.

* Proceed in the same manner to make the scale of minutes for all the other orders.

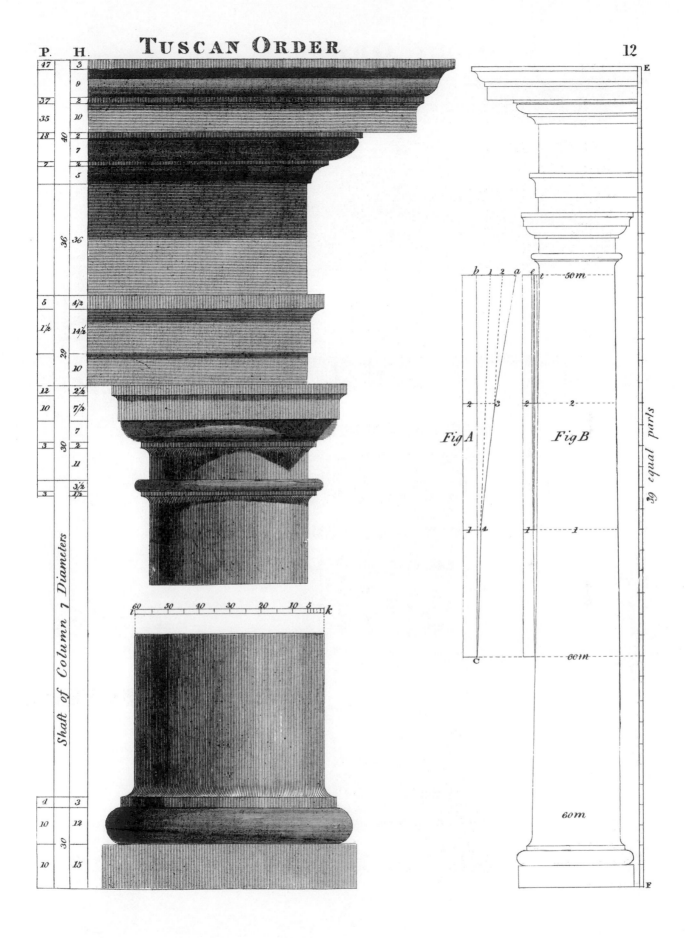

P. **H.**

P.	H.
47	3
	9
37	2
35	10
18	2
	7
7	2
	5
36	36
5	4½
1½	14½
29	
	10
12	2½
10	7½
	7
3	2
30	
	11
3	3½
	1½

Shaft of Column 7 Diameters

60	50	40	30	20	10	5

4	3
10	12
30	
10	15

l ... *k*

b 1 2 *a* *e* *t* · 50m

Fig A · 2 · 3 · 2 · 2 · *Fig B*

C · 1 · 4 · 1 · 1 · 60m

E

39 equal parts

60m

C · 60m

F

Shaft of Column 8 Diameters

PLATE XIII.

To draw the Doric order.   Divide the whole height into sixty-five equal parts, six of which are the diameter of the column, just above its base ; the column, including base and capital, is nine diameters high ; the entablature is one diameter and fifty two minutes high.

If it should be required to execute this order on a pedestal, divide the whole height into eighty equal parts, six of which are the diameter of the column ; the pedestal is two diameters and thirty minutes high, or fifteen of those parts.

If required to execute it on a subplinth, divide the height into seventy one equal parts ; give, as before, six to the diameter of the column, and one diameter to the subplinth.

A, is the plancer of a mutule ; divide g h, and e c, each into six equal parts ; also c h, and e g, each into five equal parts ; draw diagonal lines across the mutule, and through each of those divisions, the intersection of which will make the centres for drawing the bells; B, is a section of the mutule, taken from a to b, on A ;* C. is a triglyph ; divide its breadth into twelve equal parts ; give one to each half channel on the outside ; two for each space or interval ; and two for each channel, and two parts will remain in the middle ; every two divisions, or parts, is the width of a bell ; the sides of each bell, if continued, would terminate in a point at the top of the fillet above them ; D, shows the plancer, or lower end of the bells, also the under edge of the fillet above them ; E, is a section of the triglyph from o to q ; the triglyphs and mutules each, are thirty minutes wide ; the centre of one of each ought always to be placed exactly over the centre of a column ; the spaces between the triglyphs, called metopes, are always square,* and may be left plain, or enriched with pateras or oxheads, according to fancy ; when the column is fluted, it has twenty in number, and those without fillets ; to diminish its shaft, proceed as before directed in the Tuscan order.

* Triglyphs are seventy-five minutes from centre to centre.

On plate 21 is a dentil cornice which may be used instead of that with mutules, and drawn from the same scale as the rest of the order. Plate 20, fig. 4, shows the plancer of the cornice with mutules ; *d, c, a, b, e,* shows the manner of forming pannels in the plancer ; it may sometimes be necessary to make them ; but generally it succeeds best plain.

IONIC ORDER

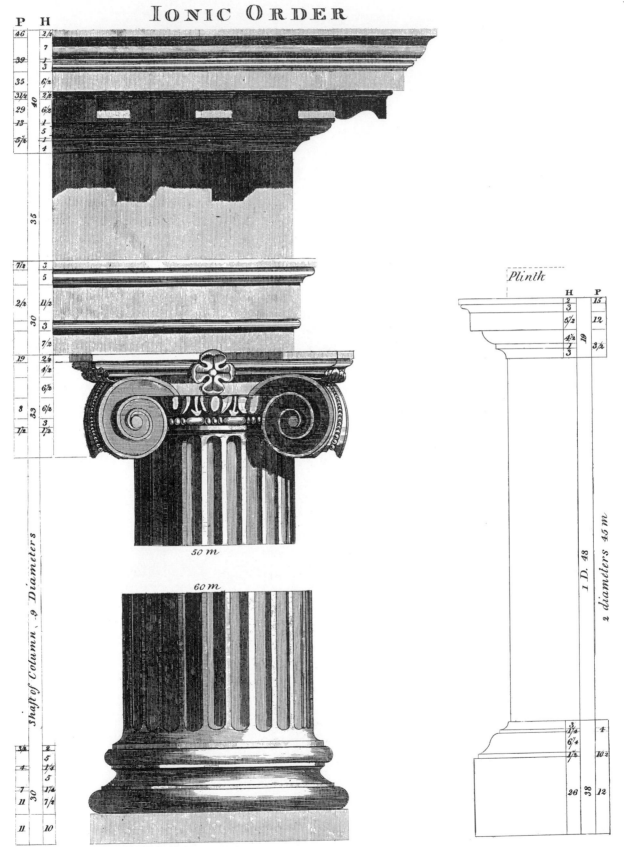

14

50 m

60 m

Shaft of Column, 9 Diameters

Plinth

1 D. 48

2 diameters 45 m

PLATE XIV.

To draw the Ionic order. Divide the whole height into forty seven equal parts, four of which are the diameter of the column, just above its base ; the column, including base and capital, is ten diameters high ; the entablature is one diameter and forty five minutes high.

If it should be required to execute this order on a pedestal, divide the whole height into twenty nine equal parts ; two of which are the diameter of the column ; the pedestal is two diameters and forty five minutes high ; if necessary to execute it on a subplinth, divide the whole height into fifty one equal parts, four of which will be the diameter of the column ; make the subplinth one diameter high ; make the modillions ten, ten and one half, or eleven minutes in front ; place them thirty one minutes from centre to centre ; always the centre of a modillion exactly over the centre of each column ; to draw the curve of the plancer, or under side of it, see plate 20.

FIG. 2, PLATE 20.

Divide a 6, into six equal parts ; on 4, make the arch 5, i, on c, which is 1 1-2 part ; from 4, make the arch i, n, on a ; with the same distance in your compasses, complete the arch, n, 1, a. Fig. 1, is the plancer of the cornice. On plate 21, is an Ionic cornice, with dentils, which may be drawn from the same scale as the rest of the order, and used instead of the modillion cornice.

PLATE XV.

To draw the Corinthian order.   Divide the whole height into twenty six equal parts ; give two of them to the diameter of the column : if, on a subplinth, divide the whole height into twenty eight parts : give two of them to the diameter of the column, and make the subplinth one diameter of the column in height : if a pedestal is to be added, divide the whole height into thirty four equal parts ; two of which are the diameter of the column ; make the pedestal three diameters of the column in height ; the entablature is two diameters high ; cornice, forty eight minutes ; frieze, forty one ;   architrave, thirty one ; capital, seventy ; base, thirty minutes ; column, including base and capital, eleven diameters.   I have given this order Palladios Ionic base for the sake of variety : but the Attic base may, with propriety, be used in all the orders, except the Tuscan ; if no enrichments are used in the frieze, it may be reduced to thirty six minutes in height ; the modillions are thirteen minutes in front, and thirty five from centre to centre.   The directions given for placing modillions, in the Ionic order, are to be strictly observed in this, and in the Composite order.

CORINTHIAN ORDER

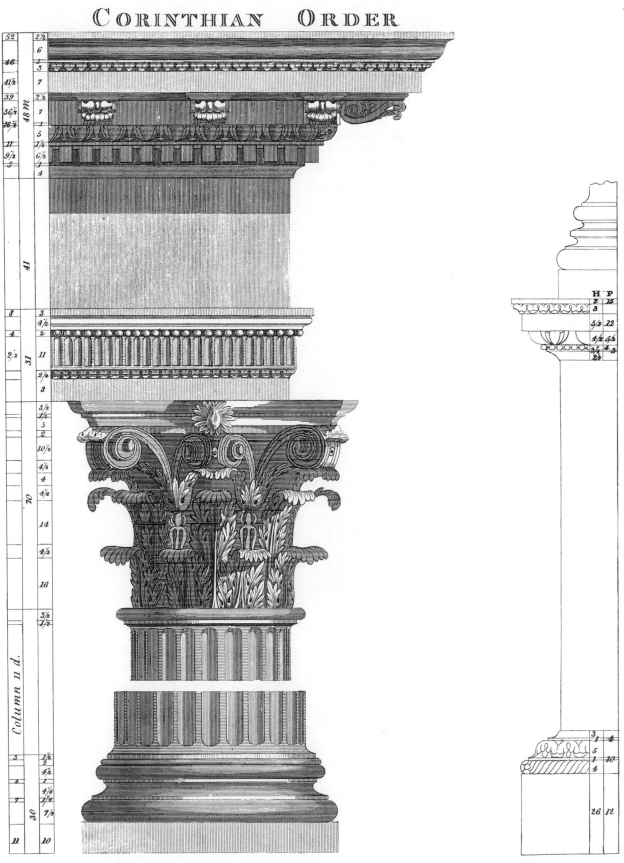

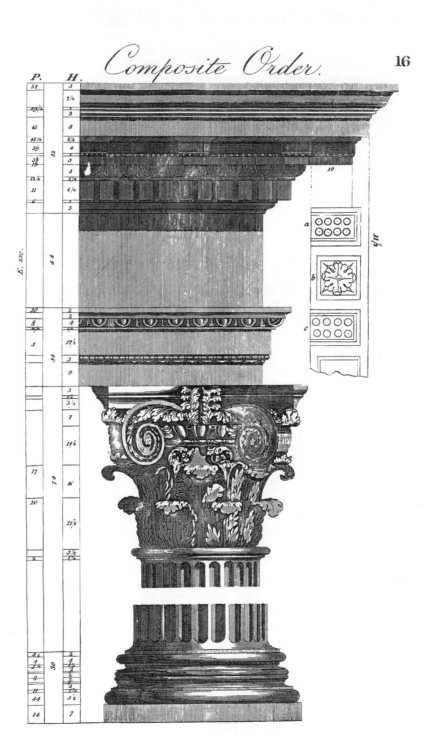

PLATE XVI.

COMPOSITE ORDER.

To draw this order, divide its height into seventy nine equal parts ; take six of them for the diameter of the column. If a subplinth be required, divide it into eighty five parts, take six as before, for the diameter ; make the subplinth one diameter. If a pedestal be necessary, divide it into ninety seven parts, take six for the diameter, give the pedestal three diameters.

The modillions are eleven and a half minutes in front, measuring on the lower facia ; and thirty eight minutes from centre to centre. Their plancer may be embellished with eight bells each, like those of the Doric mutule, see *a* and *c*.—*b* represents a pannel sunk up into the plancer between the modillions.

PLATE XVII.

MODERN IONIC CAPITAL.

FIG. 3.

Shows the mouldings, which may be turned, or worked out of a solid plank.

FIG. 4.

Shows the volute and abacus which may be made out of a solid piece of timber. Let the grain of the wood be horizontal. They may be completely finished before they are put together.

FIG. 2.

Shows the projection of the volute and abacus from the face of the column.

FIG. 1.

Shows the appearance when put together.

FIG. 5.

Is a simple way of drawing a volute; the height is twenty four minutes, which divide in twelve parts; No. 7, will be the centre of the eye; draw a square in the centre of it of the size of one of those parts; the angles, which are No. 1, 2, 3, 4, will be the four centres. This square, being divided into four parts both ways, will give four more centres, 5, 6, 7, 8, which are all that are wanted. A circle being described at the angles of the square, will be the size of the eye; from 1, on the eye, draw the line from A to B, then from 2, on the eye, draw the line from B to C, and so on until it is completed.

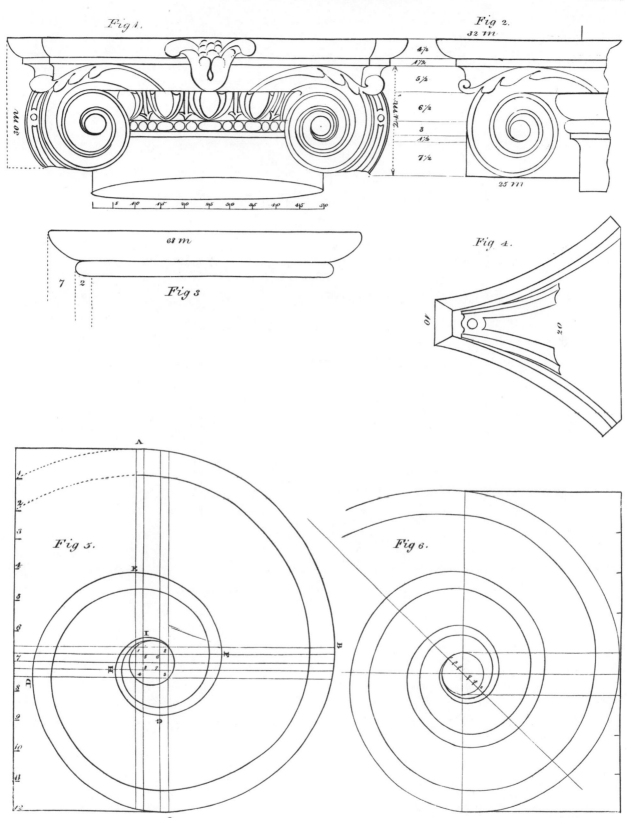

Fig 1.

Fig 2.

Fig 3

Fig 4.

Fig 5.

Fig 6.

D. Reynard Del.

Wightman Sculpt

ROMAN IONIC

Plate 18.

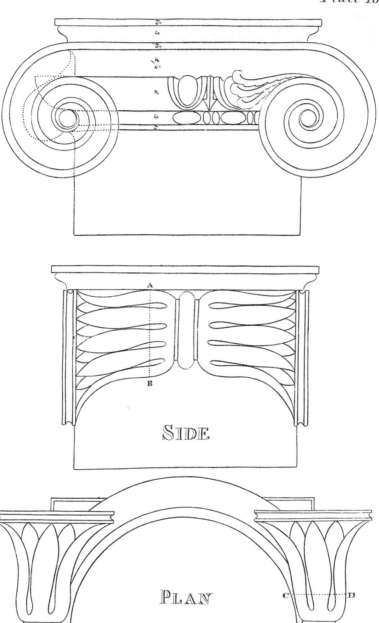

SIDE

PLAN

PLATE XVIII.

Shows the front side, and plan of the Roman Ionic capital.   The upper part of the astragal is equal in thickness, and in height, to the eye of the volute ; the height of the ovolo above, is from the upper side of the eye, to the upper side of the fillet in the second revolution ; the projection of the cincture, or hollow under the fillet of the astragal, is equal to the height of the fillet ; and the projection of the bead is a semicircle ; make the ovolo a quarter of a circle. whose projection is from the perpendicular line of the fillet.   The dotted line upon the volute, is a section through the side at A B, or through the plan at C D ; the ornamental part is drawn by hand.

PLATE XIX.

How to work the Corinthian capital. The first thing to be done is, to get out four blocks, fig. 1, forty two minutes square, and sixty one minutes long ; these being formed like fig. 2, and tacked together, will form the block ; the projection and height of all its parts may be taken from fig. 4, and drawn on the block ; after which each quarter may be wrought separate. The corners being taken off at C, fig. 2, will give an opportunity of securing it to the bench ; be much easier to get at to relieve its parts ; be in less danger of breaking ; and likewise save some time in cutting a hole through to fit on the neck of the column. The abacus may be got out of plank in four pieces, in form of A, fig. 3, and nailed, or dowelled together. The flower, in the centre, must be made separate and nailed on ; all the rest of the parts may be got from fig. 6.

PLATE XX.

Fig. 1 represents the plancer of the Ionic cornice at an external angle, Fig. 4 is also a representation of the Doric cornice, at an external angle,—$a\ b\ c$ and d are representations of pannels, which are sometimes used in the plancer of that cornice, when it is very large and near the eye, but it generally succeeds best plain.

Fig. 5 represents the plancer of a mutule of this order, which has already been explained. Fig. 2 shews the side and end view of the Ionic modillion ; to draw it, divide a 6 into six equal parts on 4 ; make the arch $5\ i$ on c, which is one and a half parts from 4 ; make the arch $i\ n$ with the same distance on n and 1 ; make the intersection at a and on a complete its curves.

PLATE XXI.

On this plate are three examples for cornices, belonging to the Tuscan, Doric, and Ionic orders. That of the Tuscan is represented with blocks, which may be used with success when small, and at a considerable distance from the eye. Those of the Doric, and Ionic, are represented with dentils, and are proper for inside finishing, &c. Draw each of them from a scale, made on the diameter of their respective columns.

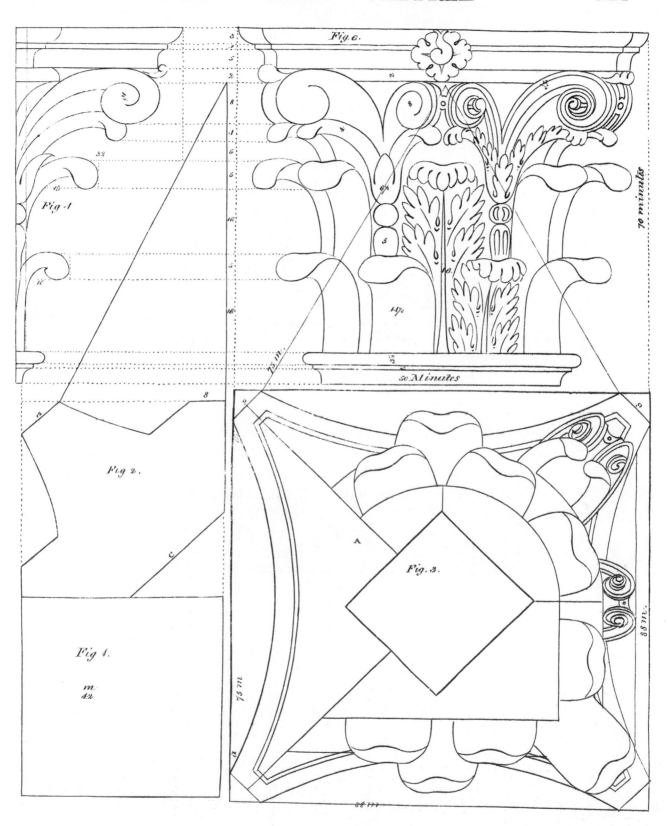

Fig. 6.

Fig. 1.

Fig. 2.

Fig. 4.

m
42

Fig. 3.

A

50 Minutes

70 minutes

88 m.

75 m.

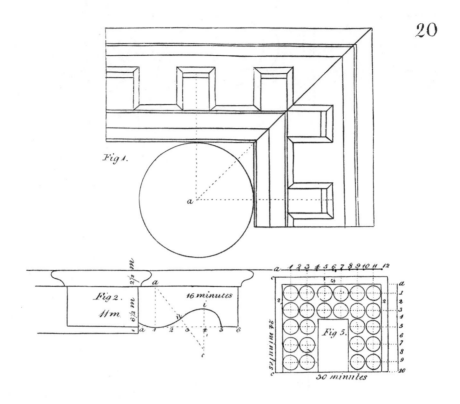

Fig 1.

Fig 2.

16 minutes

Fig 5.

30 minutes

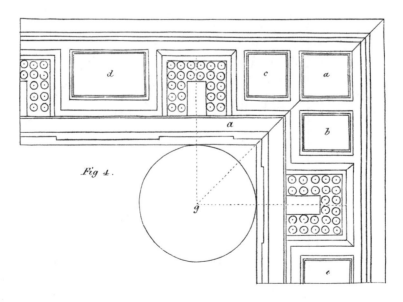

Fig 4.

TUSCAN CORNICE

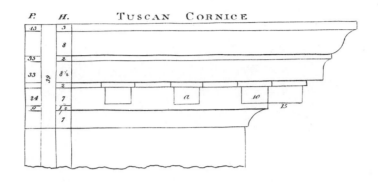

P.	H.
13	3
	8
35	2
33	8½
	2
24	7
5	1½
	7

a 10 15

H. 39

DORIC CORNICE

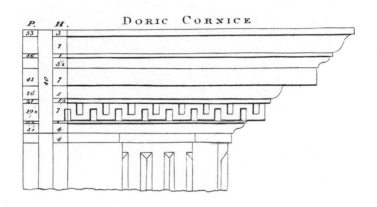

P.	H.
53	3
	7
16	1
	5½
41	7
26	5
21	1½
19½	7
16½	
5½	4
	4

H. 40

IONIC CORNICE

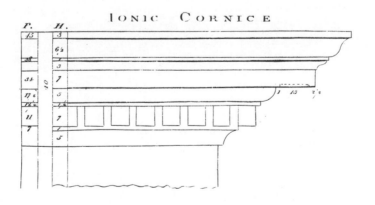

P.	H.
13	3
	6½
36	1
	3
34	7
17½	5
14½	1½
11	7
7	5

H. 40

1 13 2½

OF COLUMNS.

COLUMNS, when well disposed of, are very ornamental, and in some cases, of real use ; but care ought to be taken, that they be properly placed in such situations as they will appear to advantage ; and in such numbers, and of such size, as will best suit the building on which they are placed.

Columns, when placed within one, or one and a half diameter of each other, may be made smaller than if placed singly. There are but few places where they ought to be placed nearer to each other than one half of their diameter. When more than two are wanted, the largest opening ought to be left in the centre ; if more than four are wanted, place two of them about one diameter from each other, at each angle of the portico or building on which they are placed. When placed in front of a building, they ought to stand in front of the pier ; and never before windows or doors. When they are placed one over another, they ought to be exactly so, and the lightest on the top, as the stoutest is best calculated for support. Where one column is placed on the top of another, the diameter, at the base of the upper column, ought to be taken from the diameter of the neck of the lower one. Columns for the support of galleries in churches, should be no larger than is necessary to support the weight they have to sustain, on account of their occupying too much room in the pews, and obstructing the sight of the congregation ; they, in that case, may be from ten to twelve, or thirteen diameters high ; their entablature, taken from a scale made on their diameter. If columns be placed over them, for the support of the roof, they must be placed on a pedestal, which will continue around the front of the gallery, and ought to be ornamented with the base and cornice of the pedestal, or some other mouldings of their size, or nearly so. Avoid making the cornice of the pedestal from five to nine inches, and placing a small cornice, nearly the size the cornice of the pedestal ought to be, just above the lower columns, which awkward manner of finishing fronts of galleries is very often to be met with in churches and meeting houses, especially in country towns.

OF PILASTERS.

PILASTERS are, I believe, a Roman invention. The Greeks employed antæ in their temples to receive the architraves where they entered upon the walls of the cell. These, though they were in one direction of equal diameter with the columns, of the front, were, in flank, extravagantly thin in proportion to their height ; and neither their bases nor capitals, bore any resemblance to those of the columns they accompanied. The Roman artists disgusted, probably, with the meagre aspect of these antæ, and the want of accord in their bases and capitals, substituted pilasters in their places, which, being proportioned and decorated in the same manner with the columns, are certainly more seemly, and preserve the unity of the composition much better.

They differ from columns in their plan only, which is square, as that of the column is round. Their bases, capitals, and entablatures, have the same parts, with all the same heights and projections, as those of columns ; and they are distinguished in the same manner, by the names of Tuscan, Doric, Ionic, Corinthian and Composite. Columns are certainly the most perfect. Nevertheless there are occasions, in which pilasters may be employed with great propriety ; and some, where they are, on various accounts, even preferable to columns.

Engaged pilasters are employed in churches, galleries, halls, and other interior decorations, to save room ; for as they seldom project beyond the solid of the walls, more than one quarter of their diameter, they do not occupy near so much space, even as engaged columns. They are likewise employed in exterior decorations ; sometimes alone, instead of columns, on account of their being less expensive.

When pilasters are used alone, as principal in the composition, they should project one quarter of their diameter beyond the walls, which gives them a sufficient boldness, and in the Corinthian and Composite orders, is likewise most regular ; because the stems of the volutes, and the small leaves in flank of the capital, are then cut exactly through their centres.

When pilasters are placed behind columns, and very near them, they need not project above one eighth of their diameter, or even less ; when they are on a line with columns, their projection is to be regulated by that of the columns ; and consequently, it never can be less than a semidiameter, even when the columns are engaged as much as possible. This extraordinary projection, however, will occasion no very great deformity, as the largest apparent breadth of the pilaster will exceed the least, only in the ratio of eleven to ten, or thereabouts. But if columns be detached, the angular pilaster should always be coupled with a column, to hide its inner flank ; because the pilasters will otherwise appear disproportionate, when seen from the point of view proper for the whole building, especially if it be small, and the point of view near.

It is sometimes customary to execute pilasters without any diminution ; diminished pilasters are, however, on many accounts, much preferable. There is more variety in their form ; their capitals are better proportioned, both in the whole, and in their parts, particularly in the Corinthian and Composite orders ; and the irregularities, occasioned by the passage of the architraves, from diminished columns, to undiminished pilasters, are thereby avoided ; as are likewise the difficulties of regularly distributing the modillions and other parts of the entablature, either when the pilasters are alone, or accompanied with columns.

The shafts of the pilasters are sometimes adorned with flutings, in the same manner as those of columns ; the plan of which may be a trifle above a semicircle, and they must be to the number of seven on each face, which makes them nearly of the same size with those of the columns. The interval between them must be either one third, or one fourth of the flute in breadth.

The capitals of Tuscan or Doric pilasters, are profiled in the same manner as those of the respective columns ; but in the capitals of the other orders, there are some trifling differences to be observed. In the antique Ionic capital, the extraordinary projection of the ovolo makes it necessary, either to bend it inward considerably toward the extremities, that it may pass behind the volutes, or instead of keeping the volutes flat in front, as they commonly are in the antique, to twist them outward till they give room for the passage of the ovolo

The same difficulty subsists, with regard to the passage of the ovolo behind the angular Ionic volutes.

What has been said with regard to the passage of the ovolo behind the volutes in the Ionic order, is likewise to be remembered in the Composite; and in the Corinthian, the lip, or edge of the vase or basket, may be bent a little inward toward its extremities; by which means, it will easily pass behind the volutes. The leaves in the Corinthian and Composite capitals, must not project beyond the top of the shaft. The diameter of the capital must be exactly the same as that of the top of the shaft; and to make out the thickness of the small bottom leaves, their edges may be bent a trifle outward; and the large angular leaves may be directed inward, in their approach toward them. In each front of the Composite or Corinthian pilaster capital, there must be two small leaves, with one entire, and two half large ones; and wrought in the same manner as those of the columns are; the only difference being, that they will be somewhat broader.

The employing of half, or other parts of pilasters, that meet, and as it were, penetrate each other, in inward or outward angles, should, as much as possible, be avoided, because it generally occasions several irregularities in the entablatures.

PLATE XXII.

FIG. 1.

Is a design for a base and capital to a column, the general proportions of the capital are figured on the plate, the base and necking are composed of squares. This design may be used where fancy is to dictate, and where neither strength or great durability is required.

FIG. 2, 4 and 5,

Are designs for capitals to columns, and Fig. 3 to that of Pilasters. Their general proportions are figured on the plate, they were designed to be executed in stucco and may be used where lightness is required, and when the expences of the Corinthian capital is to be avoided.

Plate 22

Raynerd Del.

ON PLATE XXIII,

Are four designs for ornamental mouldings. If intended to be finished in stucco, they must first be modelled in clay. All the parts should be as open and free as possible, and proper leaves made to finish the mitres, both external and internal. Care must be taken to put them up perfectly straight, and not to show any joinings.

In order to model them, or any other moulding, good, fine tempered clay should be provided (pipe clay is best.) A templet must be made of wood to fit the profile of the moulding. Then run on a board, a piece of clay moulding about a foot long. This moulding may then be modelled to any pattern, and a wax mould taken of it, which will do to cast a great number of feet. In modelling mouldings, they ought to be cut as deep as possible, to give them a bold appearance, and the parts not crowded too close together. After they are cast they must be under cut, to relieve them from their ground, which will give them a rich and bold appearance.

Note. They may be a little larger than plain mouldings, and not so much quirked, for it will be difficult to take them out of the moulds.

PLATE XXIV.

OF PEDESTALS.

I have judged it more regular to treat of the pedestal as a separate body ; having no more connection with the order, than as an attic, a basement, or any other part with which it may, on some occasions be accompanied.

A pedestal, like a column or an entablature, is composed of three principal parts ; which are, the base, the dye, and the cornice. The dye is always of nearly the same figure, being constantly either a cube, or a parallelopiped ; but the base and cornice are varied, and adorned with more or fewer mouldings, according to the simplicity or richness of the composition in which the pedestal is employed ; hence pedestals are, like columns, distinguished by the names of Tuscan, Doric, Ionic, Corinthian, and Composite.

Some authors are very averse to pedestals, and compare a column raised on a pedestal, to a man mounted on stilts ; imagining that they were first introduced merely through necessity, and for want of columns of a sufficient length.

With regard to the proportion which their height ought to bear, to that of the columns they are to support, it is by no means fixed ; the ancients and moderns too, having in their works varied greatly in this respect, and adapted their proportion to the occasion, or to the respective purposes for which the pedestals were intended.

I have given the Tuscan, two diameters, fifteen minutes; the Doric, two diameters, thirty minutes ; the Ionic, two diameters, forty five minutes.; the Corinthian and Composite, three diameters each, in height; but it is not necessary to adhere always to this proportion ; it is, however, to be observed, that when pedestals are profiled under each column, and the dye is much less than a square in height, the pedestal has a clumsy appearance ; and when a pedestal of the same kind exceeds one third of the height of the column, it has a lean, unsolid, tottering aspect. But if they are continued without any breaks, this need not be

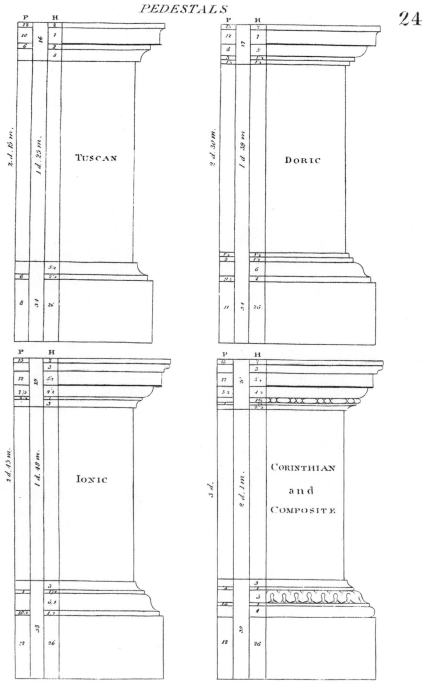

attended to ; though, indeed, there are very few occasions, in which pedestals, higher than one third of the column, ought to be suffered ; as they lessen too much the parts of the order and become themselves too principal in the composition.

The plan of the dye is always made equal to that of the plinth of the column.

It is sometimes customary to adorn dyes of pedestals with projecting tablets, or with panels sunk in, and surrounded with mouldings. The former of these practices ought seldom to be admitted, as these tablets alter the general figure of the pedestal, and when they project much, give it a heavy appearance. The latter should be reserved for large pedestals only.

With regard to the application of pedestals, it must be observed, that when columns are entirely detached, and at a considerable distance from the wall as when they are employed to form porches, or porticos, they should never be placed on detached pedestals ; for then they may indeed be compared to men mounted on stilts, as they have a very weak and tottering appearance.

PLATE XXV.

On this plate are four designs for impost mouldings.   To draw them to a given height, divide that height into twenty, or from that to twenty three equal parts, as judgment may dictate, one of which will be the height of the impost ; divide it into as many parts, as are contained in the imposts to be used ; then each member, either in height or projection, is so many parts of that division, as are figured on the plate.   The four designs for architraves, immediately above those for imposts, can also be drawn by dividing their width into as many parts as are thereon contained.

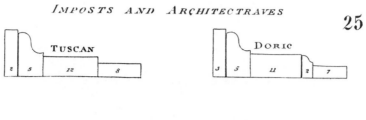

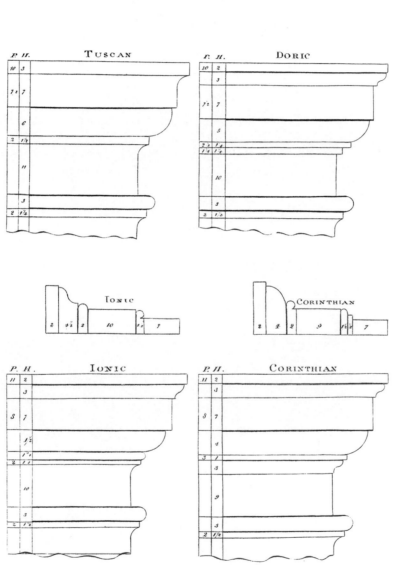

OF PEDIMENTS.

A pediment consists of a horizontal cornice, supporting a triangular, or curvilineal space, either plain or adorned, called the tympan, which is covered either with two portions of straight, inclined cornice, or with one curvilineal cornice, following the direction of its upper outline.

Pediments owe their origin, most probably, to the inclined roofs of the primitive huts. Among the Romans they were used only as coverings to their sacred buildings, till Cæsar obtained leave to cover his house with a pointed roof, after the manner of temples. In the remains of antiquity we meet with two kinds of them, viz. triangular and circular. The former of these are promiscuously applied to cover small or large bodies ; but the latter being of a heavier figure, are never employed but as coverings to doors, niches, windows, or gates, where the smallness of their dimensions compensates for the clumsiness of their form.

It is to be observed, that the cimarecta and fillet above it, of the cornice, are always omitted in the horizontal one of a pediment ; that part of the profile being directed upward to finish the inclined cornices. This difference of direction, increases the height of the cimarecta very considerably, and makes it far too large for the other parts of the entablature ; to obviate which, it will always be better, whenever the whole object is covered with a pediment, to make the profile of the cimarecta lower than usual, by which means it may, notwithstanding the increase occasioned by the difference of its direction, be made of a size suitable to the rest of the cornice. But if the inclined cornice of the pediment be, on each side, joined to the horizontal ones, the only good method of lessening the abovementioned deformity is, to give very little projection to the cimarecta ; by which means the increase in its height may be rendered very trifling.

The modillions, mutules, dentils, and other ornaments, of the inclined cornice must always answer perpendicularly over those of the horizontal cornice, and their sides be always perpendicular to the horizon.

The proportion of the pediments depends upon their size ; for the same proportion will not succeed in all cases.   When the base of the pediment is short, its height must be increased ; and when long, it must be diminished ; for if a small pediment be made low, the inclined cornice, which is always of the same height, whatever may be the dimension of the pediment, will leave little, or no space, for the tympan ; consequently, little, or no plain repose, between the horizontal and inclined cornices.   And if a large pediment be made high, it will have too lofty a tympan, and the whole composition will appear straggling, and too heavy for that which is to support it.   The best proportion for the height, is from one fifth to one quarter of the base, according to the extent of the pediment, and the character of the body it serves to cover.

The face of the tympan is always placed on a line perpendicular with the face of the frieze ; and, when large, may be adorned with sculpture, representing the arms or cypher of the owner ; trophies of various kinds, suited to the nature of the structure ; but, when small, it is much better left plain.

GRECIAN ARCHITECTURE.

TO DRAW THE ELEVATION OF A GRECIAN DORIC ORDER.

MAKE the lower diameter of the shaft of the column one eighth of the entire height of the order ; divide the diameter of the column into two equal parts, then one of these parts is a module ; divide the module into thirty equal parts, and each of these parts will be a minute ; make the height of the column twelve modules, the height of the capital one module ; divide the height of the capital into five equal parts ; give one to the hypotrachelion, and two parts to the annulets and echinus ; make the annulets one quarter of the echinus, and the remaining two parts to the abacus : make the upper diameter of the shaft three quarters of the lower diameter of the shaft ; the length of each side of the abacus two modules and one fifth, or two modules and twelve minutes ; the height of the entablature will be four modules, of which the height of the cornice will have one module, and the frize, and architrave, each forty-five minutes, or one module and a half ; divide the height of the frize into eight parts ; give the upper one to the capital of the triglyph, and the three lower for the channels ; make one edge of the triglyph in the columns at the angles of the building, directly over the axis of the column, the breadth of the triglyph twenty-eight minutes, having the other edge of the triglyph directly at the angle of the building ; and make the distance between the triglyph, or width of the metopes, equal to the height of the frize, forty-two minutes ; place all the columns between the two extreme ones, directly under the middle of the triglyphs. Make the height of the taenia one tenth of the height of the epistilium ; and the height of the regula, together with the guttae, equal to the height of the taenia. The height of the cornice being one module ; make the height of the small bead on the lower part of the cornice one minute ; the height of the mutules, including the guttae, four minutes and a half ; the length of the mutules equal to the breadth of the triglyphs, and their projection beyond the faces of the triglyphs two-thirds of their length, observing that one should be directly over the middle of every triglyph, and one over the middle of every metope ; make a fillet above the mutules one minute and a half high, to project beyond the mutules half of a minute over this fillet ; make the height of the corona one third of a module, or ten minutes, having a projecture over the fillet one minute ; make the height of the small echinus one minute and a quarter ; over the echinus, make a fillet of the same height ; over the fillet, make another echinus six minutes and a half high, and two minutes will remain for the height of the fillet above the echinus.

In order to establish the proportions and true taste of the original Doric order, the following example is taken from one of the most celebrated buildings now remaining of this order. The module is divided into thirty parts, or minutes ; the measures are all numbered in these parts ; the projections are reckoned from a line representing the axis of the column, and are figured at the extremities of each member.

PLATE A.

Elevation of the Doric Order on the Temple of Minerva, at Athens, called Parthenon.

Minerva, to whom this temple was dedicated, was the chief goddess of the Athenians. This temple is the most beautiful piece of antiquity remaining ; it was built by Pericles, who employed Ictimus and Callicrates for his architects ; the entablature is charged with historical figures of admirable workmanship ; the figures of the pediment, though seen at so great a height, appear to be as large as life, being in alto relievo, and well executed ; the figure in the middle seems to have been made for Jupiter, its right arm is broken off, which probably held the thunder ; it is likely that between his legs was placed the eagle ; for the beard and majesty, and expression of his countenance, and the figure being naked, as he was usually represented by the Greeks, sufficiently shows it to have been made for Jupiter. At his right hand is another figure covered half way down the legs, coming towards him ; which perhaps was a Victory, leading the horses of Minerva's triumphal chariot, which follows it ; the horses are finished with great art ; the vigour and spirits peculiar to these animals seems here to receive addition, as if inspired by the goddess they draw ; Minerva, in the chariot, is represented rather as the goddess of learning than of war, without helmet, buckler, or a Medusa's head on her breast, as Pausanius describes her image within the temple. Behind her is another figure of a woman sitting. The next two figures in the corner, are the Emperor Hadrian, and his Empress Sabina.* On the left hand of Jupiter are five or six figures, which appear to be an assembly of the gods, where Jupiter introduces Minerva, and acknowledges her his daughter.

The pediment at the other end of the temple, was adorned with figures, expressing Minerva's contest with Neptune, about who should name the city of Athens ; of which there only remains a part of a sea-horse.

---

* The heads of Hadrian and Sabina might have been put on one of the old figures, which was very customary among the Romans.

The frize is charged with basso relievos of excellent workmanship, on which are represented the battles of the Athenians with the Centaurs : those appear to be as old as the temple itself.

Within the portico on high, and on the outside of the cella of the temple, is another border of basso relievos round it, at least on the north and south sides, which is, without doubt, as ancient as the temple, and of admirable workmanship, but not in so high a relievo as the other ; on it are represented sacrifices, processions, and other ceremonies of the heathen worship.

This temple is now turned into a Turkish mosque.

PLATE B.

The measures in numbers.

Fig. 1.   Shewing the return of the flank at the angle of the building.   The figures in the metope are omitted.

Fig. 2.   Part of the soffit of the cornice inverted.

Fig. 3.   A section of a part of the cornice at A, fig. 1.

Fig. 4.   A section through another part of the cornice at B.

Fig. 5.   One quarter of the plan of the column.

The height of the columns is eleven modules and four minutes.   The mouldings in the entablature, and also the proportion of the column, and form of the echinus in the capital, very much resemble those of the temple of Theseus.

PLATE C.

Fig. 6.   Half of the capital to a larger size, showing the manner of drawing the echinus.

Fig. 7.   A section through the annulets of ditto, of a size much greater.

Fig. 8.   Part of a capital of the inside columns, showing the manner of drawing the echinus.

Fig. 9.   Section through the annulets of ditto, to a larger size.

PLATE C.

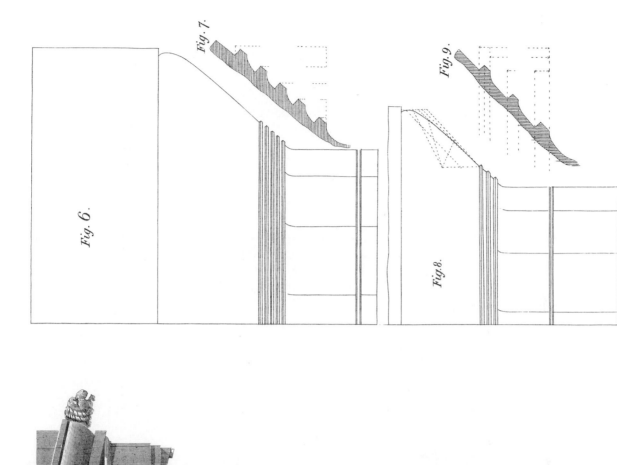

Fig. 6.

Fig. 7.

Fig. 8.

Fig. 9.

GRECIAN DORIC

PLATE B.

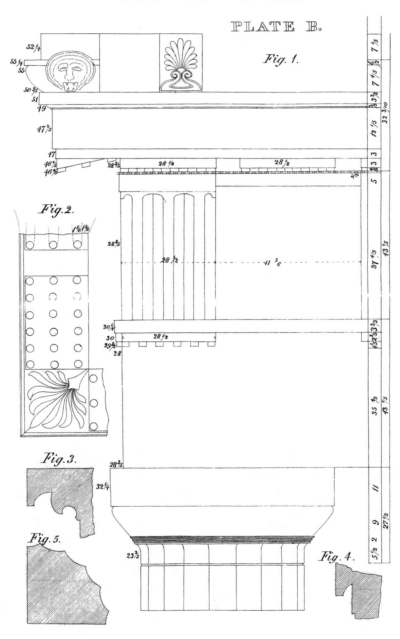

Fig. 1.

Fig. 2.

Fig. 3.

Fig. 5.

Fig. 4.

The principal parts of the Grecian Doric, compared with the Roman, and their differences.

In the cornices of every example of the Grecian Doric Order are mutules, with three rows of drops hung to their under sides ; the mutules are so distributed, that one is over the middle of every triglyph, and one over the middle of every metope ; this is a constant and uniform feature which is never omitted in the Grecian Doric ; but the cornice of what is called a Roman Doric, has no peculiar feature whatever, having in some examples mutules, and in others denteles, and is often executed without either ; neither are the mouldings always the same, but vary in different examples.

In the Theatre of Marcellus, which is the most celebrated of all the Roman Dorics, the cornice is a mixture of the Doric and Ionic ; for it imitates the mutules of the Doric cornice, which are seen underneath ; but the denteles below properly belong to the Ionic, and are the most striking features of the cornice of that order ; we find, from what has been handed down to us, of the Baths of Dioclesian at Rome, an Ionic cornice over Doric triglyphs, which is too trifling for the manly character of the Doric Order ; this erroneous practice has also been followed by some modern authors, particularly Scamozzi, and Vignola in his first example, which imitates the Theatre of Marcellus, at Rome. In the Roman Doric, the proportion of the cornice, frize, and architrave, of the entablature is found to be as the numbers, 4, 5, and 3 ; but in the Grecian, the proportion of the cornice, frize, and architrave, are as the numbers 2, 3, and 4 ; from this comparison it appears, that if the proportion of the Roman entablature were inverted, it would be much nearer to the Grecian.

In the frize of every Grecian Doric Order, two triglyphs meet together at every angle of the building ; so that the semichannel at the angle of the frize is common to both triglyphs, which are contained upon the two sides of that angle ; in what is called the Roman Doric, the middle of the triglyph* is over the axis of the column at the angle of the building, and consequently a part of a metope

* By the middle of the triglyph is meant the intersection of a vertical plane perpendicular to the front of the triglyph, dividing the triglyph into two equal parts, and also passing through the axes of the columns.

will be left on each side, next to that angle, and will have their junction at the angle of the frize, which has a very naked and unmeaning appearance, and is much more so when the frize is ornamented, for no ornament can be disposed in the semimetope, which will correspond with the metopes lying between the columns; but in the Grecian Doric, the two triglyphs next to the angle upon each side of the object meet together, by which means the angle is more finished, and all the metopes are enclosed with a border; by this means also the semimetopes are avoided.

In the Grecian Doric, the length of the metope is equal to the whole height of the frize; so that in the Grecian, it seems as if the whole height of the metope was equal to the height of the frize; and the plain part above the metopes, improperly called a part of the capital of the triglyphs, may be called, since it is the upper part of the metopes, the capital of the metopes, with as much propriety, as the upper parts of the triglyphs are called the capitals of the triglyphs; but in the Roman Doric, the length of the metope is equal to the height of the frize, excluding the capital of the triglyphs.

In the epistilium or architrave of the Grecian Doric Order, the guttae, or drops, are frustums of very acute cones approaching nearly to cylinders, and the heights of each frustum or drop never exceeds three fourths of the diameter of its base; but in the epistilium of the Roman Doric, the height of the conical frustums or drops are never less than the diameter of their base, and are always from cones whose vertical angle is very obtuse.

In the Grecian Doric, the tenia of the architrave is always in one plane; but in the Roman Doric, the tenia of the architrave under the triglyph projects forward beyond those parts of the tenia under the metopes.

In the Grecian Doric, the architrave is always a uniform plane, which gives the idea of its surface being composed of one strong beam, conformable to its use; but in the Roman Doric the architrave is sometimes divided into two heights, or facias, which gives the idea of one beam lying over the top of another, contrary to the laws of strength, as the architrave is supposed to be the support of the entablature.

In the column of every Grecian Doric Order, the abacus of the capital is always plain, being a solid parallelopiped, of which its two horizontal sides are equal squares, and its verticle or perpendicular sides are equal rectangles; the inward recesses of the annulets in the capital are in the same curve line as the

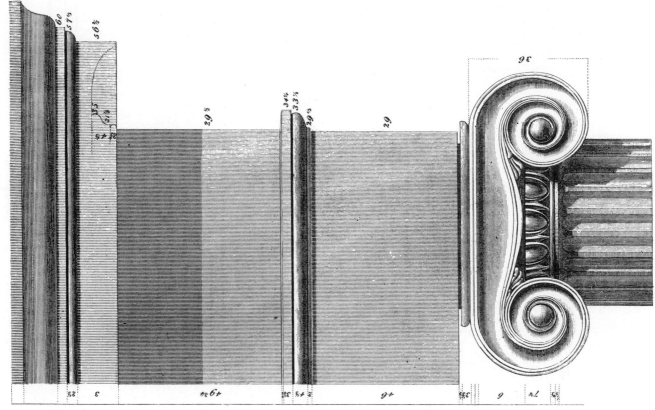

A. Bowen Sc.

A. Bowen Sc.

GRECIAN IONIC.

Fig. 2.

Fig. 1.

A. Bowen Sc.

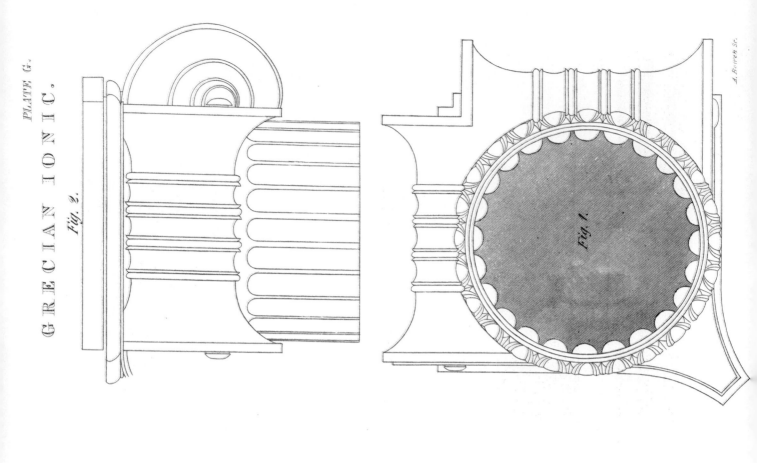

GRECIAN IONIC.

Fig. 2.

Fig. 4.

Fig. 3.

A. Bowen Sc.

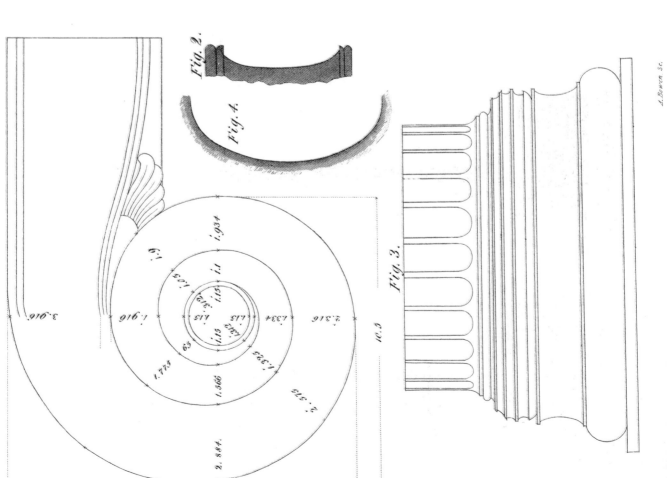

ovolo above them,* and their outward extremities are parallel to their inward recesses; the fluting of the column is always continued through the hypotrachelion, and also through the scape of the column, and terminates immediately under the lower annulet of the capital; but in the Roman Doric, the abacus is always crowned with a cymatium, and the inward recesses or angles of the annulets are never in the same curve line with the echinus, the hypotrachelion is never fluted, and the fluting of the column always terminates at the bottom of the scape under the fillet or apophygis of the column.

In the Grecian Doric, the highest columns which are to be found, are not more than 13 modules and four minutes; whereas in the Roman Doric the principal example is the Theatre of Marcellus; the height of the column is 15 modules and 21 2-3 minutes, which is too extravagant a height for columns without bases.

In the Grecian Doric the mean diminution of Doric columns is 2-9 of the bottom diameter; but in the Roman, the mean diminution of the column is between 1-5 and 1-6, or 11-12 of the bottom diameter.

PLATE D.

The Proportion of the Grecian Doric compared with the Roman, each having the same Altitude.

In this plate may be seen, at one view the difference between the Grecian and Roman Doric, where the simplicity of the Grecian, the greatness of its parts, and their beautiful arrangement, will render its application to public buildings much more advantageous than the Roman, where its numerous members make it appear poor and trifling; its columns resemble a wooden pillar, and not a strong and durable marble or stone column, capable of supporting its entablature; the multiplicity and littleness of its members renders the cornice a mass of confusion, even almost at any distance from the object: but the boldness of the Grecian Doric attracts the attention of the spectator by the grandeur and fine proportion of its parts, the form of its mouldings, and the beautiful variety of light and shade on their surfaces, which greatly relieves them from each other, and renders their contour distinct to the eye.†

* The Doric Portico at Athens excepted.

† The small parts of every object ought to appear distinct to the eye at a reasonable distance from the building; for if this be not the case, it will be labour in vain, and will greatly diminish the beauty of the building.

GRECIAN IONIC.

PLATE E.

From the Ionic Temple on the River Ilissus, at Athens.—With the proportional measures in numbers, including the entablature and capital of the columns.

The simplicity and the greatness of the parts, their judicious arrangement, the beautiful turning of the volutes, and the graceful curve of the hem hanging between them, renders this one of the most beautiful and bold examples of this Order.

The elegant base of the column, the grand proportion of the entablature, the massy mouldings of the cornice, and the spacious surface of the frize, well adapted for sculptured ornaments, and the architrave for its strength, as it is not broken into two or more facae, are considerations which should recommend this example.*

PLATE F.

From the Inside of the Portico of the Temple of Minerva, at Athens.

Fig. 1.   Volute of the capital, with the measures in feet, inches, tenths, hundredths,† &c.

Fig. 2.   A section through *a b*, fig. 1.

Fig. 3.   Base of the columns, with a small part of the step.

Fig. 4.   Section of a flute.

PLATE G.

Fig. 1.   Plan of the angular capital.

Fig. 2.   Side of the angular capital.

* This example has been executed, with little variation, by Henry Holland, Architect, on the colonade before Carleton-House; and also on the portico or entrance into Melbourne-House, Charing-Cross, London.

† Feet are marked thus, 5º signifies five feet. Inches thus 3 signifies three inches; and the decimal parts with a point before them in the usual manner.

Plate 26

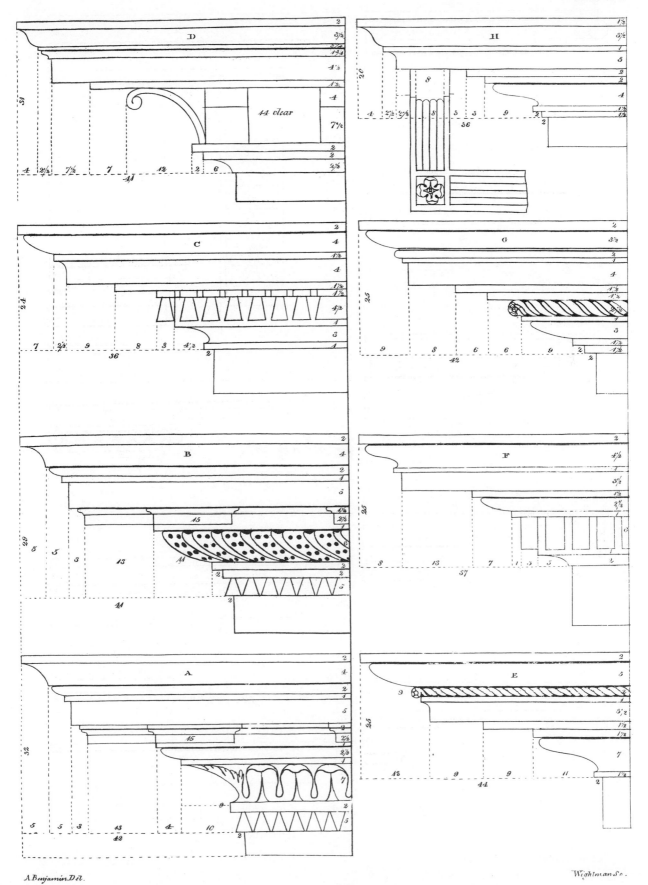

Plate 27.

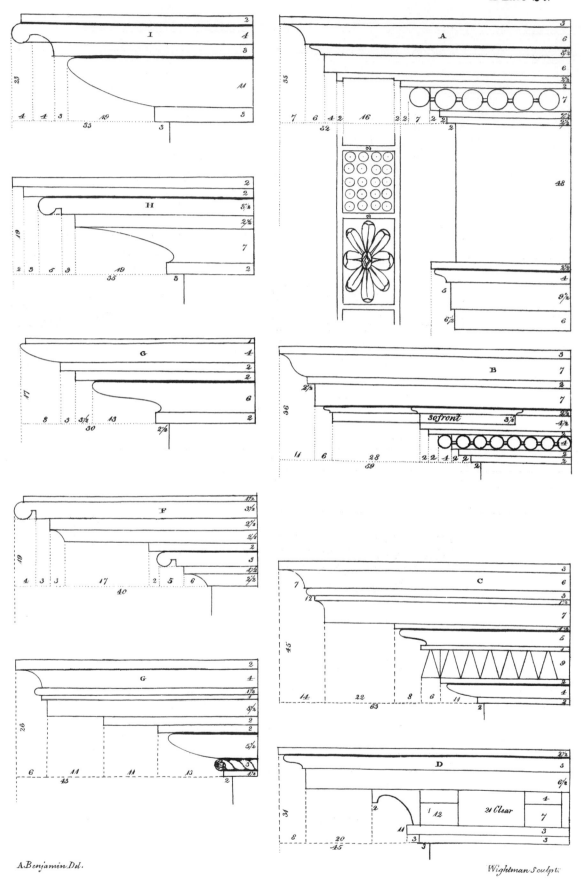

A.Benjamin Del.

Wightman Sculpt.

PLATES XXVI & XXVII.

OF CORNICES.

To proportion cornices to the eaves of buildings, divide the whole height into thirty parts, give one part to the height of the cornice.　For example, suppose a house to be thirty five feet high, divide thirty five feet into thirty parts, and one thirtieth will be fourteen inches, which must be divided into as many parts as are contained in the height of the cornice you make use of, and those parts given to the mouldings in height and projection, as figured on the plate.　It is sometimes necessary to vary the above proportion.　If it be required to proportion a cornice to a basement story house of forty feet high, and twenty five feet front, unconnected with any other building, I would advise to divide the height into forty parts, which would be twelve inches for the height of the cornice.　Again, if a house be forty feet high, and from fifty to sixty feet front, or a block of buildings from seventy five to one hundred feet front, one thirtieth may not be too large for the cornice ; and if a house of two stories high, say twenty five feet whole height, and from fifty to sixty feet front, one thirtieth would be ten inches, which would not be large enough ; in that case I would advise to make it eleven and a half or twelve inches.　A, is a copy of the original drawing for the eave cornice of that very large house which was lately built for Thomas Amory, Esq. in Park place, sixty four feet on Park street, one hundred and five on Beacon street ; walls sixty two feet high ; cornice twenty inches high, which is about one thirty seventh part of the height ; the drops, or bells, at the foot of the cornice, lie on the brick wall, so that the bricks in the interval between the drops are plainly seen, and ought not to be considered as a part of the cornice.　B C and D are intended for eave cornices and B C and D, on plate 27, are also intended for eave cornices.　The entablature

ERROR ON PAGE 64——PLATE F, IS
" From the Ionic Temple on the River Ilissus, at Athens."

A, in plate 27, is intended for frontispieces, and is drawn from the same scale of minutes as the orders, and may be used with some of their columns.   H G F E, on plate 26, and I H G F G, on plate 27, are intended for cornices for rooms, &c.   They may be made either of wood or stucco.

To proportion cornices for rooms, give the cornice one fortieth part of the height of the room.   If a room is ten feet high, one fortieth will be three inches, which is to be divided according to directions given for eave cornices.

REMARKS ON CORNICES.

As cornices make a very considerable part of architecture, there cannot be too much care taken to make them appear to as much advantage as possible, and to manage their mouldings so as to take up no more room than is sufficient to answer the purpose.

The projection of cornices, for rooms, ought to be at least one fourth more than their height ; the parts should be as few as possible, and those well pro- portioned ; not crowd in any moulding that cannot be seen.   About half of the projections ought to be given to the plancere, which will prevent its looking bulky, and give it a light appearance.   Their fillets ought not to be too small, give them a good projection before each moulding ; at least as much as they rise.   Their quirks ought to be large, as the principal beauty of plain cornices depends on the shadows of their quirks.   When mouldings are ornamented, they may be larger than when plain, as carving lightens them.   They ought never to be too much crowded with ornaments, but always leave a sufficiency of plain space to form a contrast.   Three embellishments are generally suffi- cient for any cornice, and one may be in the plancere.   Stucco cornices admit of much greater variety than wooden ones, but nearly the same rules apply to both.

28 p.

16 parts

30 p.

18 p.

16 p.

15

26 p.

17 p.

18

28 p.

18 p.

13 p.

24 p.

22 P.

12½

9

25 p.

14 p.

9

6

Observe that the ornaments be bold, and proportioned to the height of the room : not to make the same mouldings serve for a room of twenty feet high that was modelled for one of ten ; and that they always be such as will appear natural and open. In some cases where the room is low, the plancere may be laid flat on the ceiling, or even sunk level with it. Their projection may, in some cases, be double their height, and their height when enriched, with three ornaments, about a thirtieth part of the height of the room. Their projection ought, in some measure, to be conformable to the size, as well as their height, to that of the room. This will admit of no exact rule ; therefore must, in a great measure, depend on the judgment of the designer.

ON PLATE XXVIII,

Are six designs for cornices, calculated to be made of stucco. Make their height one thirtieth part of that of the room in which they are to be used, divide that thirtieth into as many parts as are contained in the cornice you intend to use, and then each member of the cornice is so many parts as are figured on the plate.

PLATE XXIX.

THREE DESIGNS FOR FRIEZES.

To model friezes for stucco, the first thing to be done, is to prepare a ground of clay, of proper size, and about half an inch thick, which must be floated perfectly even on a stiff board. The drawing of the frieze may then be laid on it, and the outlines traced with a tool or pencil, which will leave indented outlines on the clay. A sufficient quantity of fine clay may then be laid on all the parts which are to be raised, with a small trowel or tool. The artist will then exercise his own skill in embossing it to a proper degree of boldness, according to the height of the room, and the good or bad effect it may have, depends a great deal on this first emboss. This may be performed with small spear shaped tools, made of iron, wood, or bone. The fingers must do a great part in rounding, and softening its bold parts, when it is embossed, to have a proper effect. It may then be finished by smoothing it with the fingers and small tools, using a small quantity of oil. When the modelling is finished, and a mould taken off, it must be cast with plaster of Paris, and neatly undercut and relieved in all the bold parts. The cornice and architrave should be finished before the frieze is put up, and sinking made in the wall to receive the thickness of the cast, so that when finished, the ground of the frieze should be exactly over the line of the wall. The casts must be soaked before put up, and the joinings finished so as not to be seen. The same process will do for any ornament that has a flat ground.

Plate 29

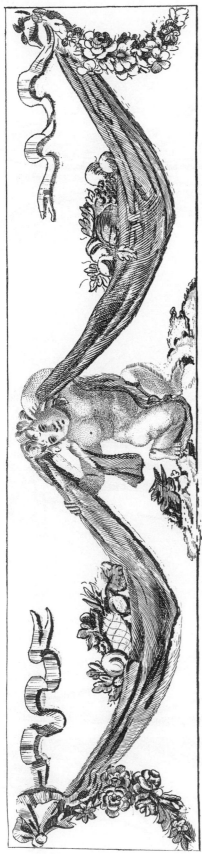

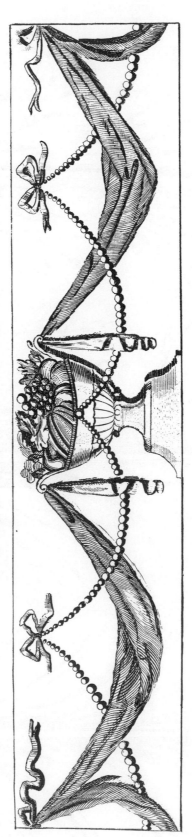

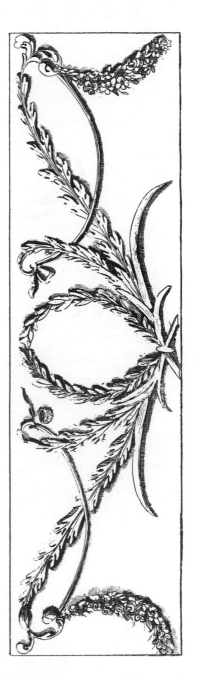

FRIEZES

Raynerd Del.

Wightman Sc.

Plate 30

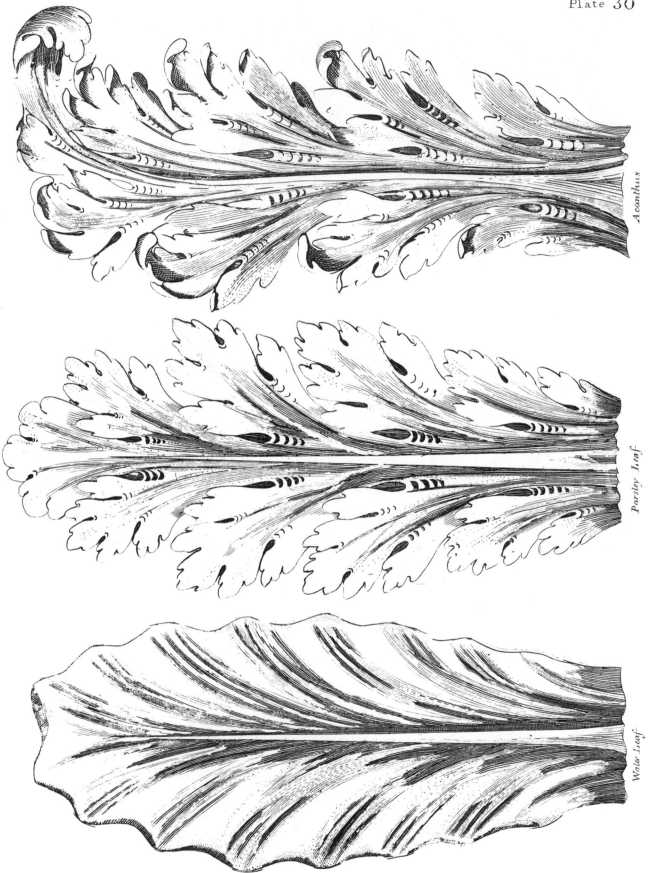

Acanthus

Parsley Leaf

Water Leaf

Raymond Del.

Plate 31

14 parts

Wightman Sc.

Fig. 2.

Fig. 1.

12 parts

D. Raymond Del.

PLATE XXX.

DESIGNS FOR LEAVES,

To be used in centrepieces for ceilings, or any other place required. The rules for modelling friezes will do here, except that they must be modelled and cast without a ground, and must be well trimmed, and made as open in the raffleings as possible.

PLATE XXXI.

FIG. 1.

Is a design for a door case, intended for inside finishing, where the room is so large as to require more than an architrave round the door. Divide the width of the door into eight equal parts ; make the architrave equal to one of them. Make the frieze and cornice equal to one seventh of the height of the door. Make the truss one twelfth of the whole height, and make the tablet one eighth of the whole height, in width, and make its length one half of that of blocking course. The side pilasters may be in width equal to the architrave.

FIG. 2.

Is a front door with only two columns or pilasters. This is intended for a situation that will not admit of more in width, and where there is sufficient height. The entablature may be of the Corinthian order, with fancy capitals of one diameter in height. Make the tablet in length equal to one half of that of the frieze.

Where there is sufficient room, and the expense not regarded, I would always recommend more than two columns, as a single column on each side of a door has but a naked appearance.

PLATE XXXII.

FIG. 1.

Is a design for a Venetian entrance calculated for a brick house, where a great deal of light is required. The pilasters may be made fifteen or sixteen diameters high; make the architrave in width the same as that of the pilasters; and the side lights in height two thirds of the height of the opening.

FIG. 2.

Is a design for a front door, calculated for a low story, that will admit of no light over the door. The whole height is seventeen diameters of the column. The blocking, course, and tablet, help to make up the deficiency of the fanlight. It will be seen, that the columns and pilasters of this door are very slender which ought generally to be the case when placed very near each other.

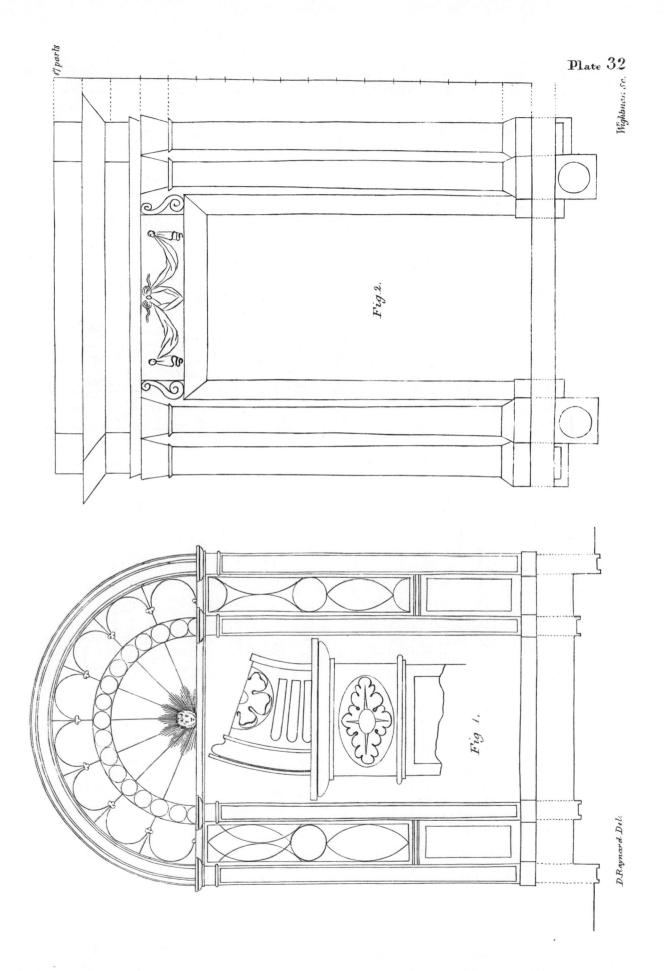

Plate 32

Fig. 2.

Fig. 1.

17 parts

Wightman, Sc.

D.Raynard.Del.

Plate 33

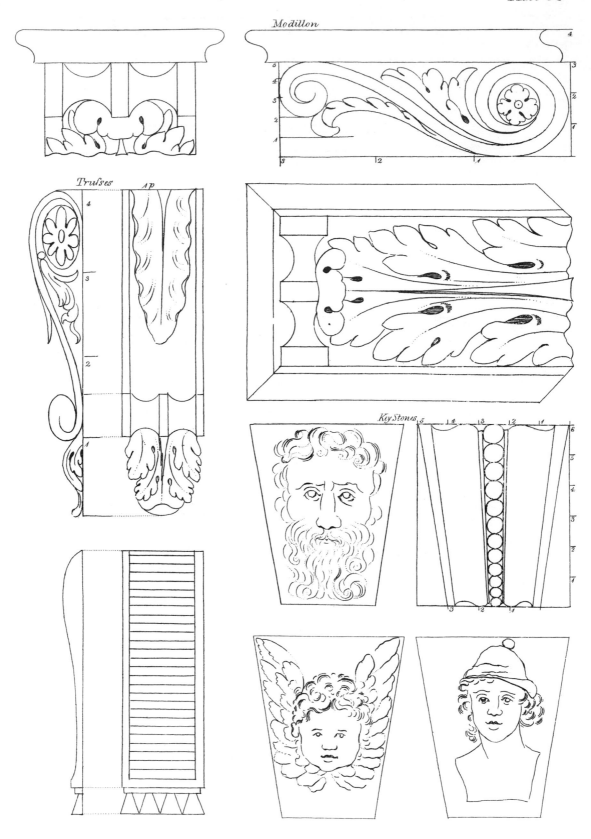

Modillon

Trusses

Key Stones

PLATE XXXIII.

Contains two designs for trusses ; four for key stones ; with a profile plan, and front of a modillion.   It would be absurd to confine the student to any particular proportions for trusses, as their situation must, in a great measure, determine their size and dimensions.   We frequently see them, and with propriety too, of every size and dimension.   I would, however, recommend them to be made with less projection than is commonly practised.   Keystones are less used now than they were formerly.   The ancients used them in almost every door or window. · This might be going to excess, but they are very useful, as well as handsome, in some situations ; serving to wedge and strengthen the arch, as well as to give its centre a bold and conspicuous appearance.   If ornamented, they ought to be bold and striking, and emblematical of the building.   Masks or heads are proper ornaments for them, if well executed.

PLATE XXXIV.

SEVEN DESIGNS FOR BANISTERS, AND FIVE DESIGNS FOR URNS.

To proportion banisters, the highest must be first found, then divide it into six parts, one of which will be the diameter ; the plinth is one half the diameter, the abacus one third.   In whatever form they are made, let them be slender at top, and stout at bottom.

Banisters, when used for balustrades, may be considered as a pedestal to an order, and the proportion may be the same.   When a balustrade is placed over an order, its height must be the same as an entablature it stands on ; there is no situation that requires them to be lower, but it is often necessary to make them higher.   The plinth of the balustrade must be placed exactly on the line of the wall ; if on the top of a house, or if on an entablature, it must be perpendicular over the frieze.   We frequently see balustrades project out as far as the nose of the cornice, but this is a very bad and unnatural practice, for should another order be put on such a balustrade, it would break down the cornice.

Urns admit of a great variety of forms, and when well executed will be very ornamental in their proper places, but they ought not to be used in every situation.   The ancients used them to deposit the ashes and bones of the dead, and for sacred uses only ; and while the mind is impressed with these ideas, it cannot be pleasing to see them in every situation.   Their use ought to be principally confined to monuments, wall pieces, churches, mausoleums, mourning pieces, &c. &c.

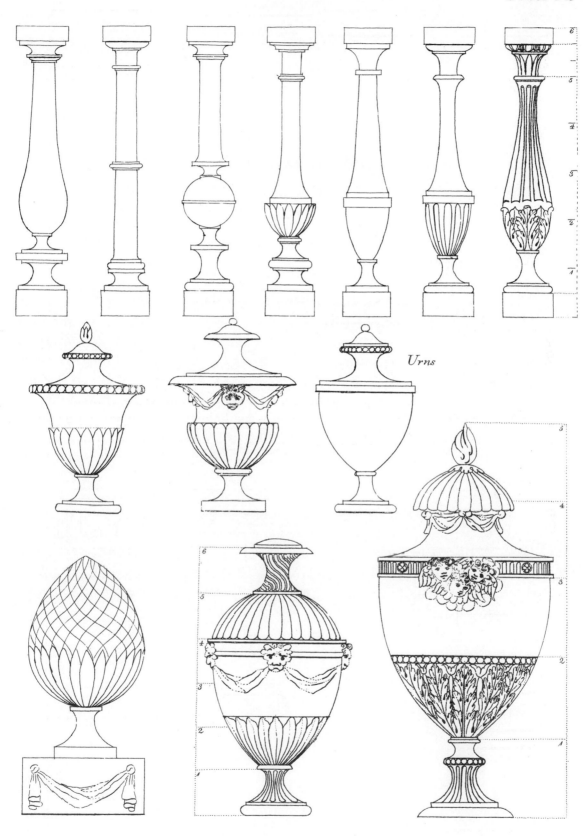

Urns

D. Raynard Del. *Wightman Sc.*

Plate 35

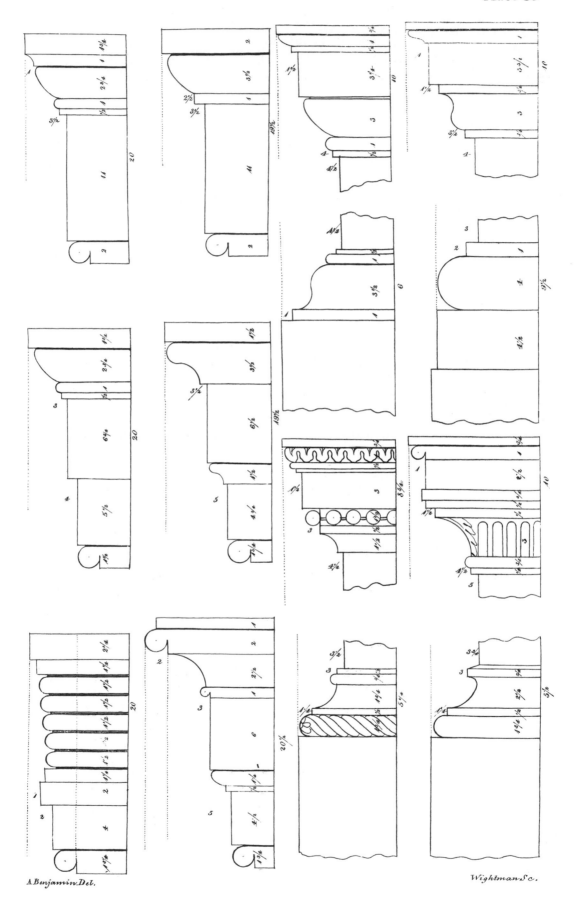

PLATE XXXV.

EXAMPLES FOR ARCHITRAVES, BASE AND SURBASES.

To proportion base and surbase mouldings to the pedestal part of rooms, divide from the floor to the top of the surbase into ten parts, give one to the height of the surbase. Suppose the height from the floor to the top of the surbase to be two feet eight inches, one tenth would be three inches and one fifth of an inch which divide into as many parts as are contained in the height of the surbase you make use of, and those parts given to the mouldings in height and projection, as figured on the plate. The same scale, or parts, will draw the base mouldings in proportion to the surbase ; let the plinth be from five to six inches wide.

To proportion architraves to doors and windows, divide the door into eight parts, give one to the width of the architrave. If a door is three feet six inches wide, one eighth would be five and a quarter inches. Divide five and a quarter inches, into as many parts as are contained in the architrave you make use of, and those parts given to the moulding as figured on the plate. It is very often necessary to vary this proportion, and oftener for inside of windows than for doors. For example, if a door is three feet six inches wide, the opening between the architraves to the windows of the same room, would probably be as much as four feet four inches ; one eighth of which would be six and a half inches, which would be very improper, as you would have two widths of architraves in the same room. I therefore should advise to make the architrave to the window five and a quarter inches. Again, if a door should be six feet wide, one eighth of it would be nine inches, which would be too large, and may be reduced to six and a half, or seven inches. Some judgment should be exercised respecting the situation in which architraves are to be used. If they are on external parts of buildings, and at a considerable distance from the eye, it will be proper to make them larger than if used on internal finishing, and near to the eye.

PLATE XXXVI.

Are six designs for ornamental stucco ceilings, with some of their parts enlarged.

It was not my intention when I first began this work, to lay down any rules for ornamental stucco work, but merely to give a few examples by drawings; but as it has never before been attempted, to my knowledge, and my principal aim being to explain those parts of architecture which have been overlooked by others, and willing to give the student every information in my power, although it is the most difficult branch in architecture to learn, and still more so to instruct; yet I hope the following hints will be of some use to those who are young in the business, and be no injury to those who are well acquainted with the art of stucco working. When a ceiling or walls of a room are to be ornamented, the first thing to be done after the size, height, and form are known, is to draw a design; after which, all the parts are to be drawn at large. When this is done, and the plastering finished, which should be floated perfectly even, there are two ways of executing it on stucco work, the first is by what is called laying it on by hand, which is modelling it on the ceiling with stucco,* with small iron or wooden tools. This kind, if executed in a masterly style, is to be preferred; but where workmen cannot be got to execute it, or its expense is too great, the parts may then be modelled in clay, and moulds taken from them, and the ornaments cast with plaster of Paris. Though this is not the best method, it is much less expensive, and requires less skill to perform it; and if well managed will have a very good effect. In ornamenting ceilings, the figure should be of a proper boldness and strength of shadow to the height of the room, and be significant of its use. They ought to be such as will appear ornamental, or they had better be left out; and those parts which were cast with grounds be sunk level with the line of the

---

* The stucco is made of lime putty, mixed with pulverised marble, or raw plaster of Paris, with sometimes a little white sand and a little white hair, to prevent it from cracking. The mixture is then put on a dry brick wall for twenty four hours, after which it is taken off and well beaten, and put on again. This is repeated for four or five days, when it will be fit for use. This preparation makes it tough, and prevents it from cracking.

ceiling, or they will have a heavy appearance.   When a room is low, all the parts of the ornaments should be correctly finished, with very delicate strokes, and light in proportion to the height ; yet to preserve a proper boldness of tint. When a room is very high, there may be bold and well placed strokes, without regard to a great deal of delicacy.   The principal object is to show a sufficient quantity of shadow, to give it a rich and bold appearance, without having the parts too large and heavy.   A ceiling may sometimes be panelled to advantage, but ought not to be laid out in too many geometrical figures.   Regard ought to be paid to the use of a room, as it is as easy to introduce emblematical subjects as those void of meaning.   An ornament, however well executed, is not fit to be put in every room.

Those that would be exceedingly well adapted to a dancing room, for instance, would be ridiculous if put in a church or a courthouse ; or those modelled for a drawingroom or a bedroom, would not be fit for a diningroom or a hall.

In ornamenting a dining room, there may be introduced grapevines, wheat, barley, or fruit of any kind ; cups, vases, &c. or any thing that denotes eating or drinking ; but care must be taken to group them in some graceful form.

In a drawing room, foliage, wreaths, festoons, or baskets of flowers, with myrtles, jasmines, convolvalus, roses, &c. displayed with taste, and in a lively manner.   Every subject that is introduced, ought to approach as near to nature as art will admit of.   A hall, saloon, or staircase, ought to exhibit something of more solidity and strength.   Therefore trophies of different kinds may be introduced, and not so highly ornamented as the rest of the house.   I would not recommend the last mentioned apartments to be finished higher than the Doric order, if regard is paid to any.   It is to be remembered that objects are not to be dispersed about a room without order, but should be grouped into trophies, with a great deal of judgment, and care taken to give them as easy and natural an appearance as possible, and introduce nothing that will look stiff or mechanical. To imitate nature requires a great deal of art.   A trophy of love may be composed of **cupid's bow** and quiver, hymen's torch, doves or a wreath of roses, myrtles or **jasmines**, &c. &c.   A trophy of music ; harps, violins, flutes, hautboys, **music book**, French horn, with laurel branch, &c.   A trophy of war ; drums, fifes, trumpets, swords, battleaxes, fascine, colours, palm branches, &c. or any warlike implement.   A trophy of peace ; a caduceus, doves, olivebranch, a sword, burning, &c. &c.   A trophy of **commerce** ; the anchor and rudder of a ship, bales, trunks, cornucopias, with **other** articles of commerce. A trophy of navigation ; anchors, cables, rudders, **mariners'** compass, speaking trumpet, quadrant, pendant, &c. &c.   A trophy **of** agriculture ; wheat corn, scythes, sickles, rakes, forks, flowers of any kind, &c. &c.

Raynerd Del.   Wightman Sc.

PLATE XXXVII.

Contains eleven designs for chimney pieces ; some of which are plain, and some ornamental. Care should be taken, however, not to overload them with ornaments, as they are exposed and liable to be broken. The proportion of chimneypieces I am obliged to leave to the judgment of the workmen ; for, in my opinion, no exact rule can be laid down that will answer for every room. A room, however small, must have a fire place large enough to be useful, and should the same proportion be used in a room twenty feet high, and large in proportion, it would be so large as not to look well, and be too high in the opening for the smoke to ascend without spreading into the room. It will be found by Count Rumford's experiments, that the nearer the throat of the chimney is to the fire the better the draft. The smallest opening should never be less than two feet nine inches in height, and the largest ought not to be higher than three feet two inches, but two feet eleven inches will be found to be a useful height for common rooms, and the width may be about four feet.

PLATE XXXVIII.

OF DOORS AND SASHES.

A is a design intended for an inside door. To proportion the frieze panel, divide its width into four parts ; give three of them to the height of the panel. All the other parts are figured in feet and inches on the plate.

B is a design intended for an outside door ; divide the width of the frieze panel into five parts ; give four of them to its height. Outside doors ought to be two inches thick, and never less than one and three quarters. Inside doors ought to be the last mentioned thickness, they ought not in any case be less than one and one half inch in thickness.

C D E and F, are designs for sashes ; and are intended to be placed over either inside or outside doors. Their small bars may be made of either wood, iron, or pewter.

Plate **38**.

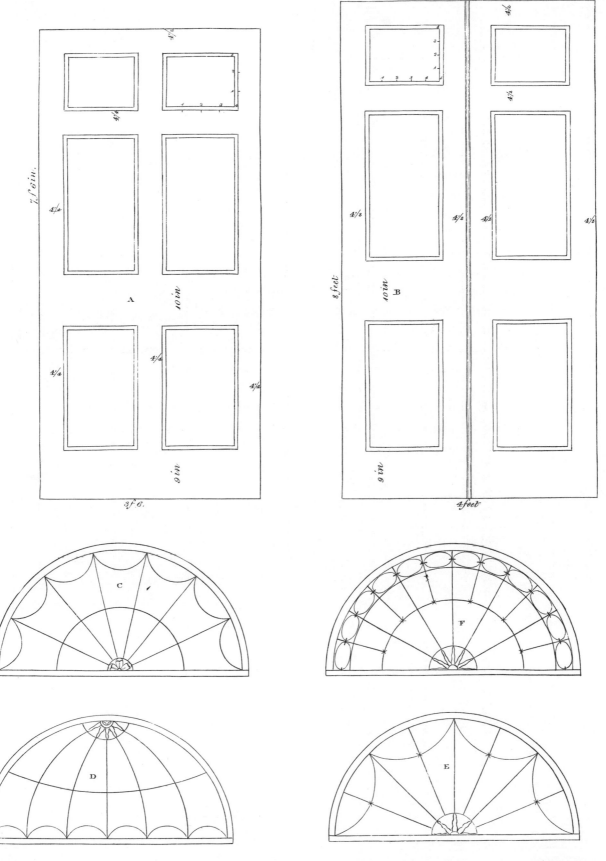

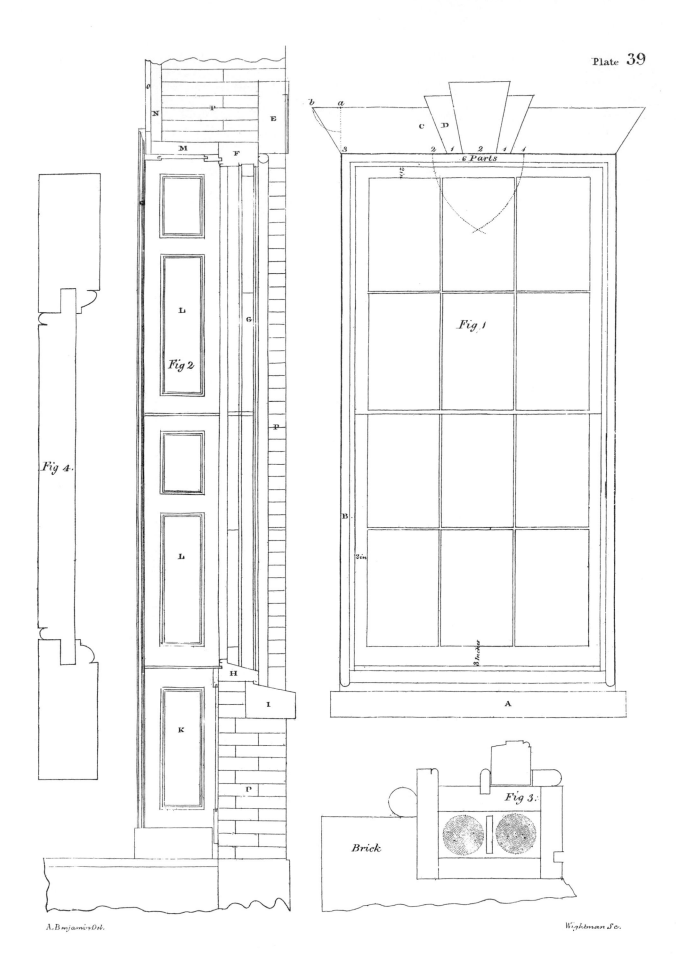

Plate 39

Fig 1

Fig 2

Fig 4

Fig 3

Brick

6 Parts

A. Benjamin Del.

Wightman Sc.

PLATE XXXIX.

OF WINDOWS, &c.

FIG. 1.

Shows the manner of setting a sash, frame stone cap, and sill, into a brick wall.   To find the size of the keystone and bevel of the ends of the cap, divide the lower edge of the cap into three parts, and the middle third into six parts ; give two to the centre part of the keystone, and one to each of its wings, with the distance 1 2 ; make the dotted circular lines 1 and 2 ; intersect, which is the centre for drawing the edges of the keystone.   Take one half of the line 3 a and set it to b ; draw the line 3 b, which completes the bevel of the cap.

A Face of stone sill.

B Bead round sash frame, from one inch to one and a half inches in diameter.

FIG. 2.

Is a section of fig. 1, taken from the top of the stone cap to the floor of the house.

E Section of stone cap.

F Section of cap to sash frame.

G Face of pulley stile.

H Section of sill to sash frame.

I Section of stone sill.

K Elbow.

L L Shutters.

M Section of lintel over windows.

N Section of plank furring on brick wall.

O Section of plastering.

P P P Section of brick work.

FIG. 3.

Section of sash frame, set in a brick wall.

FIG. 4.

Section of stiles, panel, and mouldings of a shutter.

PLATE XL.

FIG. 1.

s Section of cap to sash frame.

r Section of soffit.

h Inside bead.

g Parting bead.

a Outside lining.

FIG. 2.

Section of sill to sash frames, &c.

h Inside bead.

g Parting bead ; the shaded part between *h* and *g* is a section of the bottom rail of the sash.

a Outside lining.

t Section of sill to sash frame.

v Section of back under window.

u Section of bead, tongued into sill of sash frame.

FIG. 3.

Section of the meeting rails of the top and bottom sash, with the side eleva‧ tions of th e upright bars.

G E and F are plans for upright bars.

FIG. 4.

Is a section of a sash frame shutters, back lining, rough furrings, plastering grounds, and architrave.

a Section of outside casing.

b Section of pulley stile.

c Section of inside lining.

d Section of back lining, next to bricks.

e Section of p arting strip.

f f Section of weights.

g Section of parting bead.

h Section of inside bead.

i Section of sash stile.

k and *l* Section of shutters.*

m Section of back lining of the boxing, tongued into the ground.

n and *c,* inside lining

o Section of architrave.

p Section of plank furring.

q Section of plastering.

   A B I and H mouldings at large for shutters.   C and D mouldings at large for doors.

---

* This hinge that hangs the shutter *k* to the inside lining *c,* ought to have one half of its thickness let into the inside lining *c,* which, by mistake, is not represented on the plate.

Plate 40.

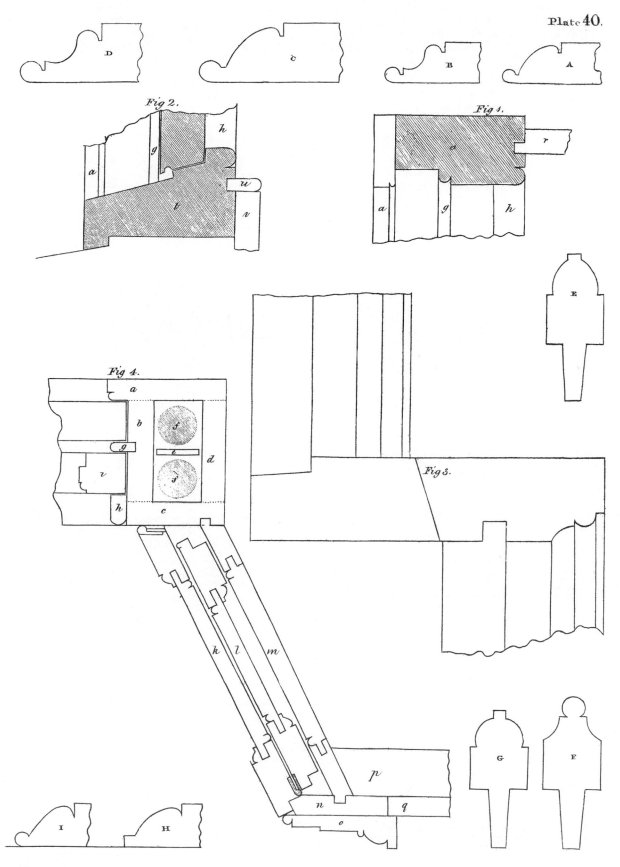

D

C

B

A

Fig 2.

Fig 1.

E

Fig 4.

Fig 3.

G   F

I   H

Plate 41

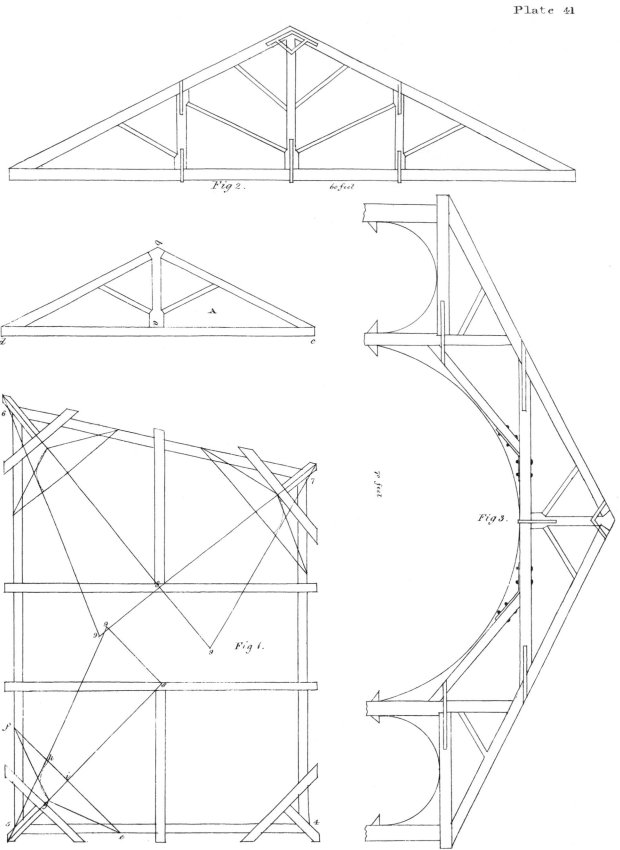

Fig 2.

60 feet

A

d   c

Fig 3.

70 feet

Fig 4.

6

7

9

8

8

f

h

i

s

e

4

A Benjamin Del.

Wightman Sc.

PLATE XLI.

FIG. 1.

Is a plan for a roof. 4, 5, 6 and 7, are the corners or angles of it. Suppose *a b* on A to be the height or pitch of the roof. To find the length of the hip rafter, draw the base line of the hip from the angle, 5 to 8, on the centre of the beam ; then set up the height of the pitch to 9, and at right angles, from 8, 5, and draw the line 9, 5, which is the length of the hip. To find the backing of hips, draw the line *e i h f* at right angles from the base line of the hip, place one foot of the compasses at *i*, extend the other to *h*, and turn it round to *g*, draw the lines *g e* and *g f*, which gives the backing of the hip. This method will give the backing of any hip, square, or bevel.

FIG. 2 *and* 3.

Are examples for principal rafters, &c. for roofs ; that of fig. 2, if well put together, will be sufficiently strong if the bearing should be extended to eighty feet, fig. 3, must have two columns for the support of each pair of principal rafters.

PLATE XLII.

FIG. 1.

Shows a form in which a roof may be framed, where you wish a dome to rise above the level of the plates.   I have made use of this example, where it had seventy feet bearing, without the least settlement.*

FIG. 2.

Shows how to find the length, width, and curve of a soffit, to fit a circular headed window, standing in a circular wall ; divide the arch from c to 12 its base, into any number of parts, as here into 12 ; draw lines through it, and continue them across the wall B, on which the window is to stand ; make e, c, in D, equal in length to the stretch of the arch A, from c to 12 ; divide $e\,c$, in D, into the same number of parts as the line 12 c in A is divided into ; transfer c 2, 3 4, 5 6, 7 8, 9 10, 11 12, &c. in B to D ; and from B to D, transfer a 2, c 4, e 6, g 8, i 10, and o 12, the thickness of the wall, and through their points trace the edges of the soffit.

FIG. 3.

Shows how to find the different curves for the edges of boards to cover a dome.   Fig. 3, the dome ; divide it into as many parts as you have boards ; g, b, c, d, are plans of four boards, with their edges in the right form to bend round the dome ; through 1 and 2, also 2 and 4, draw right lines, until they meet at a, which is the centre for drawing the edges of the first course of boards, g ; proceed in the same manner to find the centres for drawing the edges of b, c, and d, which are at c, o and e.

---

* This design has been frequently used since the publication of the second edition of this book where it had from seventy to seventy-eight feet bearing, and has answered my expectations in every instance.

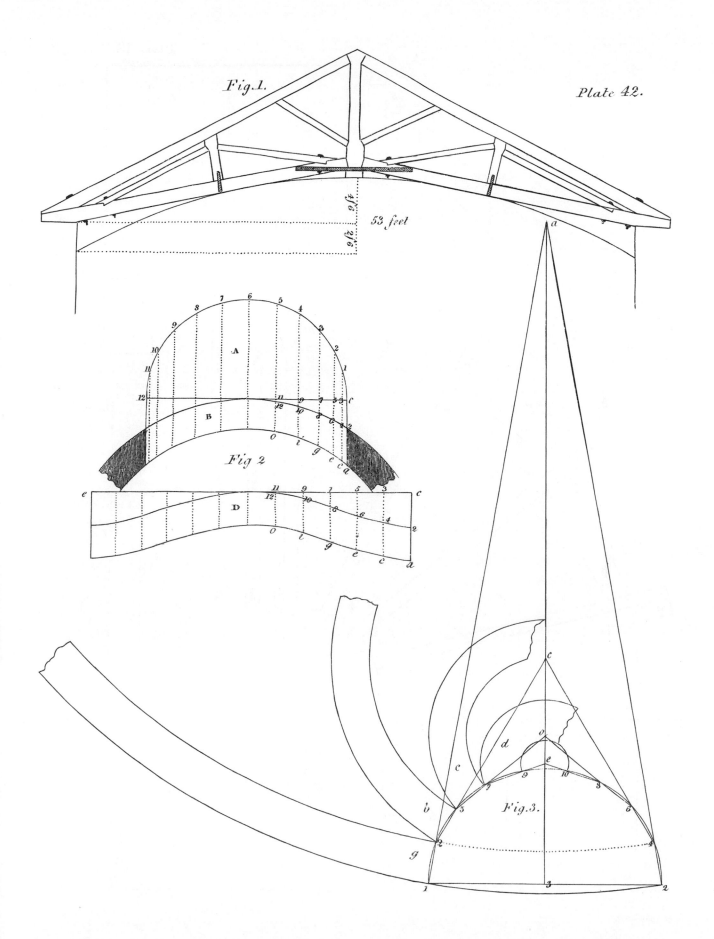

Fig.1.

Plate 42.

53 feet

A

B

Fig 2

D

Fig.3.

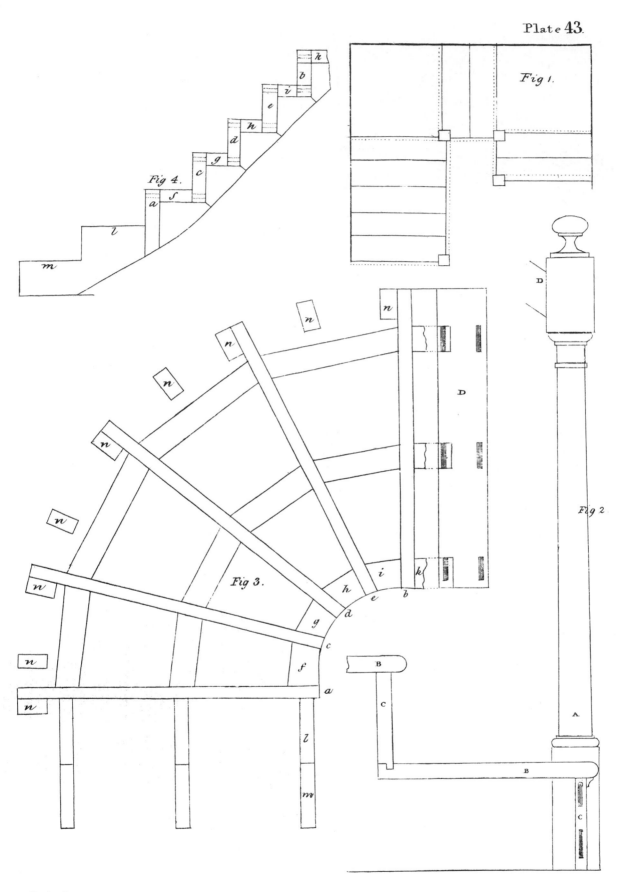

Plate **43**.

Fig 1.

Fig 4.

Fig 3.

Fig 2

A.Brujamin Del.

Wightman Sc.

PLATE XLIII.

DESCRIPTION OF STAIRS.

FIG. 1.

Shows the manner of placing newels. They always ought to be placed so as to cause the extreme part of the nosing of the step to be flush with them, as they are represented by the dotted lines on the plate.

FIG. 2.

A Is a newel for a plain staircase. D Side view of hand rail. B and B Sections of steps. C and C Section of risers.

FIG. 3.

Shows the manner of framing carriages to circular stairs. $a\ c\ d\ e\ b$ are the ends of the plank riser. D is a side view of a plank riser. The shaded parts are the mortaises to receive the tenons of k, &c. $n\ n\ n\ n\ n\ n\ n\ n$ are sections of open plank partition.

FIG. 4.

Is an elevation of fig. 3, with the circular part stretched out. $a\ c\ d\ e$ and b are the end views of the plank risers, and $f\ g\ h\ i\ k$, side views of $f\ g\ h\ i\ k$, in fig. 3, the dotted lines show both mortaises and tenons to $a\ f\ c\ g\ d\ h\ e\ i\ b$ and k. $l\ m$ are the sections of a stringboard made of plank, of which $l\ m$ in fig. 4 is a side view.

PLATE XLIV.

DESCRIPTION OF STAIRS.

HOW TO DRAW THE SCROLL OF A HAND RAIL TO ANY NUMBER OF REVOLUTIONS.

FIG. A.

Draw a circle from the centre y, G 15 14, L K J I H, about three and a half inches in diameter, and divide the circumference into eight parts ; at the points G 15 14, L K J and H through all those points, and from the centre y, draw lines 0, 4, 1, 5, 2, 6, 3, 7.   Suppose that y o is the distance you intend the centre of the scroll to be from the beginning of the twist ; from o draw p perpendicular to o G on o, with the distance o G, make the quarter of a circle, p G.   Now suppose it were required to make two revolutions in this scroll ; and, since every revolution contains eight parts, there will, of course, be sixteen in two revolutions ; therefore divide the quarter circle p G into sixteen equal parts, and draw lines from each of those sixteen divisions, parallel with o p cutting o G at 1, 2, 3, 4, 5, 6, 7, 8, 9, 10, 11, 12, 13, 14 and 15 : at y place one foot of the compasses, and extend the other to 1 on G o ; make a point with the foot, which falls on 1, at 1 on the outside of the rail ; still keep one foot at y, and take the distances y 2, y 3, y 4, y 5, y 6, y 7, y 8, y 9, &c. and prick them down at 2, 3, 4, 5, 6, 7, 8, 9, &c. on the outside of the rail.   To draw the curve, draw the line a a parallel to o y, which is the beginning of the twist ; and about two inches from the line o y, take the distance o y in your compasses, and place one foot at 1, on the outside edge of the rail, and intersect the line a a at a, which is the centre for drawing the curve a 1.   Take the distance 1 y in the compasses ; place one foot at 2, and intersect the line 1 a at b, which is the centre for drawing the curve 1, 2.   Take the distance 2 y, and from 3, intersect the line 1 a at c, which is the centre for drawing the curve 2, 3.   Take the distance 3 y, and from 4, intersect the line 2 b at d, which is the centre for drawing the curve 3, 4.   Take the distance 4 y, and from 5, intersect the line 3 c, which is the centre for

Plate 44.

Riser

Nosing

Nosing

Nosing

Bracket

Nosing

B

A

D

E

C

A Benjamin Del.

Wightman Sc.

drawing the curve 4 5, and so on, until the whole is drawn round to 14, which completes the outside curve. To draw the inside, set off the thickness of the rail on the line *a a*, and take the same centres which the outside was drawn from. The curtail step is also drawn from the same centres as those of the rail.

TO DRAW THE FACE MOULD.

FIG. B.

Make *h f* parallel to 2 6 on fig. A, and make *f g* equal to one riser ; and draw lines from *g h*, cutting the lines *h f* and 2 6 on fig. A at right angles, to the outside scroll *i j k l m n*, &c. then continue those lines at right angles from *h g*, as far as the whole breadth of the face mould ; make the line 2 6, on B parallel to *h g* ; then transfer the distances from the line 2 6, on A, to the line 2 6, on B, *i i, j j, k k, l l, m m, n n*, &c. and from those points, trace the curve line of the scroll, which completes the face mould.

TO DRAW THE FALLING MOULD.

Make the pitch board C ; make *e d* equal to the tread of one step, and *d* 6 equal to one riser ; divide *d* 6 in six parts, and draw the line 1 *a f* 3, and make 1 *a* equal to the distance from the face of the second riser to the beginning of the twist ; make *a* 3 equal to the distance from *a*, on A, where the twist begins, to 3, where the rail becomes horizontal ; divide *f* 7 on C, into seven parts, also *f* 3 into seven parts, and by intersecting the lines 3 *f* 7, the curve of the top rail is given.

TO DRAW THE INSIDE FALLING MOULD.

The inside falling mould, D, is drawn in the same manner as the outside falling mould, C, excepting its being shorter, which is occasioned by a difference of length between the inside and outside of the twist part of the rail.

In practice, the above mould should be drawn on and cut out of pasteboard, which will bend round the rail.

E is a design for nosing to steps, full size for practice.

PLATE XLV.

HOW TO FIND THE RAKING, OR FACE MOULD.

Place your pitch board, *a b c*, in fig. D ; then draw ordinates across the scroll, at discretion, and take the length of the line *d b*, with its divisions, on the longest side of the pitchboard, and lay it on *d b*, in E ; then the ordinates being drawn in E, it will be traced from fig. D, as the letters direct.

HOW TO FIND THE PARALLEL THICKNESS OF STUFF.

Let *a b c*, be the pitchboard, in F, and let the level of the scroll rise one sixth, as in the last plate ; and from the end of the pitchboard at *b*, set from *b* to *d*, half the thickness of the baluster, to the inside ; then set from *d* to *e*, half the width of the rail, and draw the form of the rail on the end at *e*, the front *b*, being where the front riser comes ; then the point *e* will be the projection of the rail before it ; then draw a dotted line to touch the nose of the scroll, parallel with *c b*, the longest side of the pitchboard ; then will the distance between this dotted line and the under tip of the scroll, show the true thickness of stuff, which is nearly five inches and a half ; but there is no occasion for the thickness to come quite to the under side ; if it come to the under side of the hollow, it will be quite sufficient, as a little bit glued under the hollow, could not be discernible, and can be no hurt to the scroll ; therefore, a piece about four inches and a half will do.

FIG. A.

Is a scroll of a smaller size, drawn in the same manner, and with the same centres as the others are, but with a centre less. The method of finding the raking mould, and thickness of stuff, is the same as fig. D.

Plate 45.

This show's how a Scroll is to be got out of the Solid

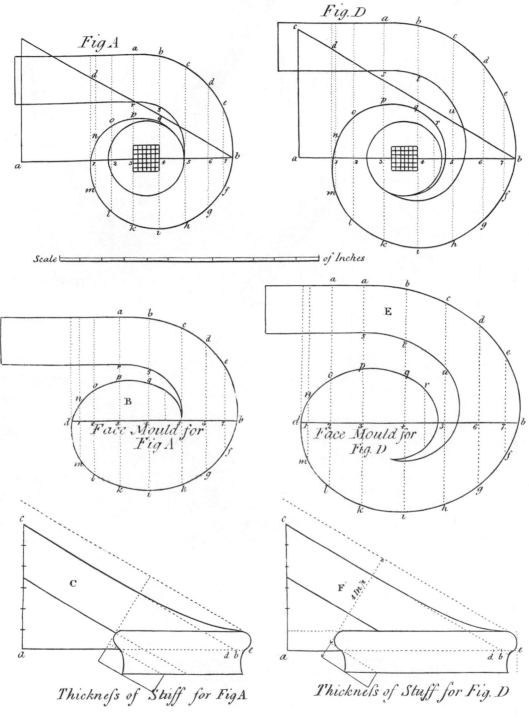

Fig. D

Fig A

Scale ┝━━━━━━━━━━━━━━━━┥ of Inches

B

Face Mould for Fig A

E

Face Mould for Fig. D

C

F

Thickness of Stuff for Fig A

Thickness of Stuff for Fig. D

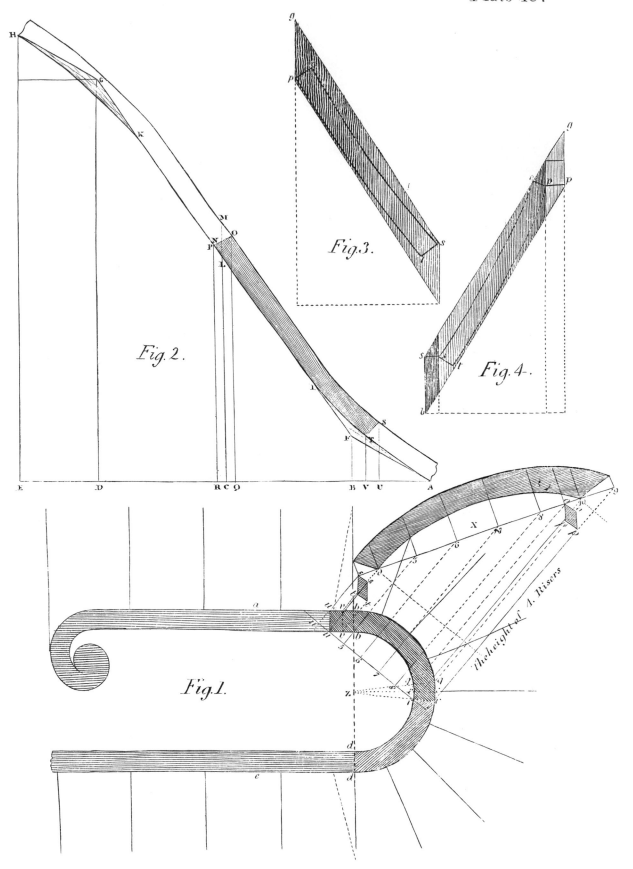

Plate 46.

Fig.3.

Fig.4.

Fig.2.

Fig.1.

The height of 4. Risers

PLATE XLVI.

TO FIND THE MOULDS FOR MAKING BUTT JOINTS FOR A RAIL, WHEN GOT OUT OF THE SOLID.

Let fig. 1 be the plan of a rail, *b c d* and *b c d*, the two sides for the circular part ; *a b*, and *d e*, the breadths of two common steps, at the beginning and end of the winders ; make the whole stretchout of the straight line, A B C D E, fig. 2, equal to *a b c d e*, round the outside, going upward, fig. 1 ; that is make A B, in fig. 2, equal to *a b*, fig. 1 ; the last common step in the ascent before the winders ; B C D, in fig. 2, equal to the circumference of the semicircular part, *b c d*, fig. 1, and D E, in fig. 2, equal to *d e* ; on the outside, fig. 1, the first common step immediately after ascending the winders, draw the lines B F, D, G, and E H, perpendicular to A E ; make B F, equal to the height of one step ; make D G, one step higher than the number of winders that is in the example ; suppose the circular part to contain eight winders, then D G, will be equal to the height of nine steps ; make E H equal to the height of ten steps ; then join A F, F G, and G H, and describe the parabolical parts A I, and K H, and the under edge of the falling mould will be completed ; the upper edge will be formed by drawing a line parallel to it, equal to the thickness of the rail. Bisect the stretchout of the circular part B D, at C ; from C, draw C M, perpendicular to A E, cutting both edges of the falling mould at L and M ; bisect L M, at N, and through N, draw O P, at right angles to the falling mould ; cutting it at O and P ; through the points, O and P, draw O Q, and P R, each perpendicular to A E, cutting A E, at Q and R ; let S T be the joint on the straight part ; then from the point S and T, draw S U and T V, perpendicular to A E, cutting it at U and V, then take the distances C R and C Q, in fig. 2, and apply them in the middle of the circular part, fig. 1, from *c* to *r*, and from *c* to *q*, and draw to the centre *r* Z, and *q* Z, cutting the inside of the rail at *r* and *q* ; also take the distances B V, and B U, fig. 2, and apply them from *b* to *v*, and from *b* to *u*, fig. 1 ; then draw *v v* and *u u* at right angles to the rail, cutting the other side at *v* and *u*; then through the points *u* and *r*, on the inside of the rail, fig. 1, draw the chord *u r*, then from all the points, *u, u, v, v, q, q,* and *r, r,* draw lines *u u s, u s, v t, v t,* and *q o,* &c. each perpendicular to the chord line *u r*; then complete sections of the rail *t t s s,* and *o o p p,* as are shown at the shadowed parts, and draw the chord line, *s o,* to touch these sections without cutting them ; then take any number of intermediate points, as 5, 6, 7, 8, in the chord *u r,* and draw the lines, 5 5, 6 6, 7 7, 8 8, perpendicular to *u r,* cutting the chord of the face mould, *s o,* at the points 5, 6, 7, 8 ; continue the lines *u s* and *r p,* till they cut the chord line of the face mould, *s o,* at *o* and 9 ; through all the points, *s, o,* 5, 6, 7, 8, 0, 10, 9, draw lines perpendicular to the chord of the face mould, *s o,* for ordinates, points being found in each of them corresponding to these ; on the plan and lines being traced through these points, the face mould X, will be completed in the usual manner.

N. B.   The small letters on the sections of the face mould, and similar capital letters on the falling mould, show corresponding places in each.

HOW TO CUT THE JOINTS.

The stuff must first be cut out by the face mould, and the joints made exactly plumb, according to the face mould, as is shown by fig. 3 and 4.

To make this appear plain, of fig. 3 and 4, are different views of the solid rail, got out by the face mould X. Fig. 3, shows the top and convex side of the piece, which is to make the rail ; take the distance 9 *p,* from the chord line of the face mould, down the perpendicular, fig. 1, and set it from 9 to *p,* in fig. 3 ; then apply the shadowed part of the falling mould at fig. 2, which is to correspond to the block of the rail, fig. 3 ; that is, apply the point S, the upper edge of the lower end of the falling mould at fig. 2, to the point *s* at fig. 3, and bend the falling mould round until the point P, the lower edge of the upper end of the falling mould, coincide with the point *p* ; draw a line all round by the falling mould ; it will show how to cut off the ends of the rail, and will also give the upper and lower edge of the rail.   Fig. 4, shows the concave side of the piece, in order to show the ends, having similar letters of reference as before.   From s in fig. 4, draw $s\ s$, at right angles to $s\ b$; then cut off the end through the line $s\ s$, as is shown at fig. 3, and through the points $s\ t$, as is shown at fig. 4.   The upper joint will be found in the same manner; that is, by drawing the line $p\ p$, at right angles to $9\ p$; then cut off the end, through the line $p\ p$, in fig. 4, and through $p\ o$, as is shown in the other view, fig. 3.   If great accuracy is required in squaring the rail, make an inside falling mould, which apply the under edge of the upper end to the point p, in fig. 4, and the upper edge of the lower end of the falling mould, to the point s, and draw lines above and below, by the two edges of the falling mould, and it will give the form of the upper and under edges of the rail.   By this method of proceeding, the workmen will be enabled to cut out the stuff of a hand rail with very great accuracy.

PLATE XLVII.

TO FIND A FACE MOULD OF A RAIL FOR A LARGE OPENING ON A LEVEL LANDING.

Let fig. A be the plan of rail; through the centre of c, draw the diameter $s z$, and produce it to A; also produce the side of the rail out to 2; then take the diameter $z s$, put the foot of the compasses in y, and cross the line A z at A; through A and y draw the line A 2, cutting the side of the rail produced at 2: then the distance from z to 2, is half the arch line of the rail; take the distance z 2, and place it on the right line $v v$ at G, on each side of w, to v, and v; draw v B, and v C, each perpendicular to the right line v v, and equal to the height of a step; draw the hypothenuse v C, and the common pitchboards, v B D, and C E F, at each end; make v H equal to v D, and c G equal to c F; and ease off the angles, G C F, and D v H, by the common method of intersecting lines, which will give the curve of the under edge of the falling mould; draw a line parallel to it equal to the thickness of the rail, will give the upper edge; produce the line $v v$, out to y, from the middle w, of the line $v v$ at G; make w y equal to w y, at the plan, fig. D; y being the place of the joint upon the plan, draw the line y 2 1, perpendicular to v v, cutting the upper side of the falling mould at 2, and the under side at 1; from 1, draw the line 1 6, parallel to v v, cutting the line 8 w, produced at 6; draw the tangent line M L, parallel to the chord a b, draw any number of indefinite perpendiculars, observing to draw a perpendicular through every joint, as from the joint d q and b y; then take the distance 1 2 from your falling mould at G, and set it from M to o, of the plan at B; also from L make L N o, equal to 6 7 8 at G; then the shaded parts at N o, and M o, are sections of the rail; then draw a line o b, to touch the corners of the section at o and b; at the points o, a, d, e, f, g, h, b, and p, draw perpendiculars to o b; then C, being pricked from the plan at B, as the letters direct, will be the true face mould.

Plate 47.

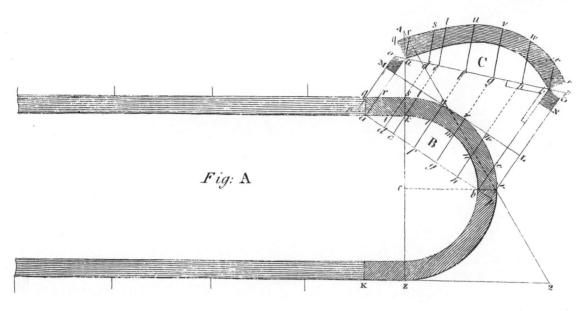

Fig: A

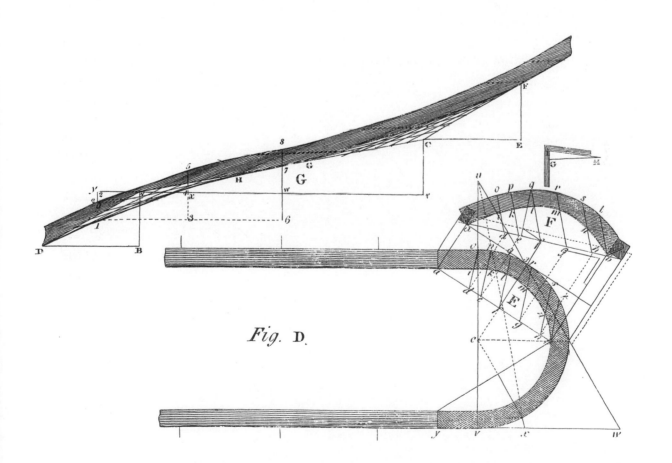

Fig. D

FIG. D.

Is a plan of the same size, showing the face mould at F, when sprung, which will be a very great saving of stuff, and not much trouble in laying it down when properly understood. This method will be clearly explained in the following pages.

PLATE XLVIII.

TO DRAW THE FALLING MOULD OF A RAIL, HAVING A QUARTER SPACE IN IT :
THENCE TO FIND THE FACE MOULDS OF THE CIRCULAR PART.

At the plan fig. A, *a c* is the stretchout of half the circular part of the rail, found thus ; divide the radius into four equal parts, and set three of the divisions out to 3, and draw a line from 3 to *b*, cutting the side of the rail produced at *a* ;* from the point *f*, in the right line *h g* at B, make *f h* and *f g*, each equal to the stretchout of half the rail, that is, equal to *a c*, fig. A ; draw the perpendiculars *h o*, *f l*, and *g t*, at B ; apply the pitchboard of a common step at F ; through the point *t* draw *t k*, parallel to *g h*, cutting the line *f l* at *k* ; from *k* to *l* set up the height of the winders ; through *l* draw *l n*, parallel to *g h*, cutting the line *h o* at *n* ; from *n* make *n o*, equal to the height of a step, for the quarter space upon the landing which only rises one step ; draw the hypothenuse *l o* ; again, draw *o p* parallel to *g h*, and *p g* ; perpendicular to *o p* draw *r p* ; then *o p q* is the pitchboard of another common step above the winders ; then these angles being eased off by the method of intersecting lines, the falling mould will be completed ; make *f u*, and *f v*, from *f*, equal to *a d*, fig. A, that is the stretchout from the middle of the arch at *b*, to the joint ; draw *v x* and *u z* parallel to *f l* ; then take the heights from 1 to *y* and *z*, and set them from A to B, and *c* will give the section, B C ; then take *m l* from the falling mould, and from D, make D E equal to it, will give the section D E ; then take *w x* from B, and make F, G at E equal to it ; from *u* draw *w r*, parallel to *g h*, cutting *f m* at *r* ; from *r* take the heights from *m* and *l*, and set up these heights from H to 1, and K at E, it will give the section I K ; then the face moulds up D and E will be traced as before directed.

* The line *a c* is nearly equal to the semicircumference, and is the most exact of any that has ever been shown by a geometrical method ; it may be depended on in practice.

Plate 48.

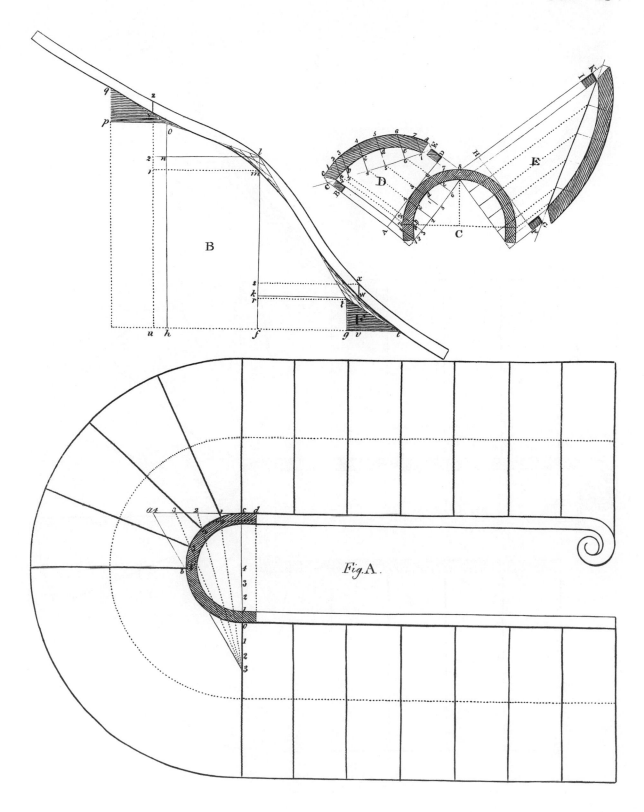

Fig. A.

Plate 49.

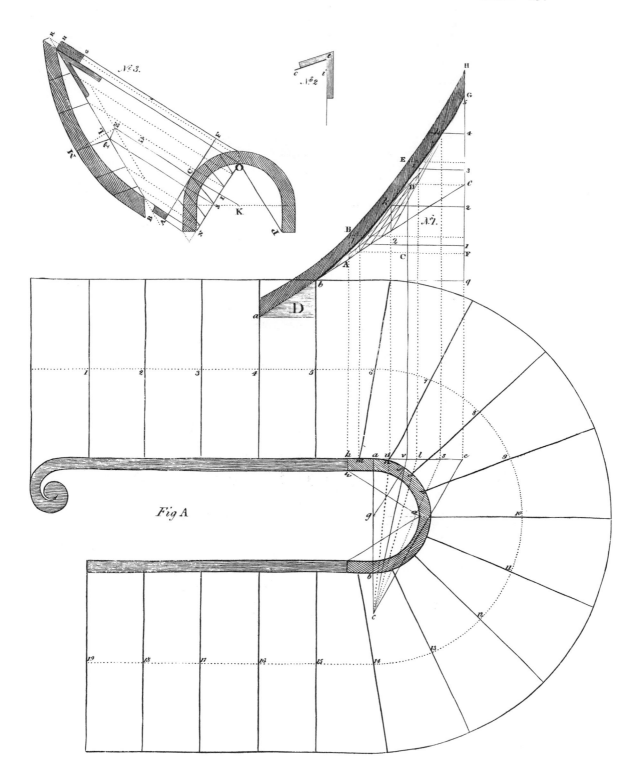

Fig A

PLATE XLIX.

THE TREAD OF A WINDING STAIR BEING GIVEN, ROUND THE MIDDLE AND THE PLAN OF THE RAIL, TO DIMINISH THE ENDS OF STEPS AT THE RAIL, SO THAT THE BALUSTERS SHALL BE REGULAR OR OF EQUAL HEIGHT WHEN FINISHED.

Let the first winder begin about the first step before the circle of the rail at D; from a to e, in the plan, fig. A, is the stretchout of half the circular part of the rail; the method of finding has already been explained in the foregoing plates; from e, draw e H perpendicular to the side of the rail; by reckoning round the dotted line from 5 to 10, you will find there are five treads, or five winders; therefore from q to 5, set up the height of five steps; produce the longest side, $a\,b$, of the pitchboard D, to c; bisect $b\,c$, at 2; draw a line from 2 to 5; then divide 2 b and 2 5, each into the same number of equal parts, and intersect the angle by the common method of intersecting lines, will give the under edge of the falling mould; then a line drawn parallel to it, the thickness of the rail, will give the upper edge, which is the falling mould for half the rail; draw the lines 1 l, 2 k, 3 i, and 4 h, parallel to $b\,q$, to intersect the falling mould, at the points h, i, k, l; from these points draw the parallel dotted lines to q H, down to the rail at $s\,t\,v\,u$; from c draw $c\,s, c\,t, c\,v$, and $c\,u$, cutting the arch line of the rail, m, n, o, p, will give the ends of the steps at the rail; then draw lines from m, n, o, p, through 6, 7, 8, 9, will be the plan of the steps.

TO FIND THE FACE MOULD OF A RAIL, SO THAT IT MAY BE GOT OUT OF THE LEAST THICKNESS OF STUFF POSSIBLE.

Lay down the plan of the rail at any convenient place, as No. 3; draw the chords of rail, N O, and O P, from the centre K, draw K E, perpendicular to the chord N O, cutting the outside of the rail at C; in the same manner draw the chord $w\,a$, at the plan, fig. A; from the centre g, draw $g\,f$, perpendicular to it, cutting the outside of the rail at f; from c draw a line $c\,f$, to cut the tangent line at v ; draw a line v E, parallel to q H ; from the joint of the rail at h, draw h B also parallel to q H ; intersecting the under side of the rail at A, and the top side at B ; draw from A, a line A F, parallel to $b\,q$; from F at No. 3, make F G H equal to F G H, at No. 1 ; from C, at No. 3, make C D E, equal to C D E, at No. 1 ; and make A B, at No. 3, from A, equal to A B, at No. 1 ; draw a line B R, for the chord of the mould to touch the shaded sections, perpendicular to N O, and A F ; from E draw E M perpendicular to B R ; make $c\,i$, at No. 2, equal to C I, at No. 3 ; make $i\,e$ perpendicular to $c\,i$, equal to E L at No. 3 ; make L M equal to $c\,e$ at No. 2 ; from E draw E T, parallel to A F, cutting chord line B R at T ; from the points T and M, draw the line T M, then T M will be one of the ordinates ; all the other ordinates are drawn at discretion parallel to it.

The reader will take notice, that before the face mould at No. 3 can be applied, the edge of the plank must be first bevelled according to No. 2 ; then the plumb line will be drawn on the bevelled edge of the plank, by the bevel that is drawn at No. 3.

Note.—By this mode of proceeding, a three inch plank will almost be sufficient for any rail of this kind, however it may ramp ; whereas in many cases, by the common method, it may require a plank of five or six inches thick. Many other advantages will attend the setting out of this plan ; I shall mention one or two.   In fixing the banisters, they will be all regular, and the stringboard will be as easy as the rail itself ; the skirting will also be quite regular ; for the ends of the steps are wider and wider as they go round to the middle of the semicircle ; lastly, a blacksmith may put an iron rail with very little trouble, the banisters being all regular ; whereas, no other plan will admit of it, unless it be set out in this manner.

Plate 50.

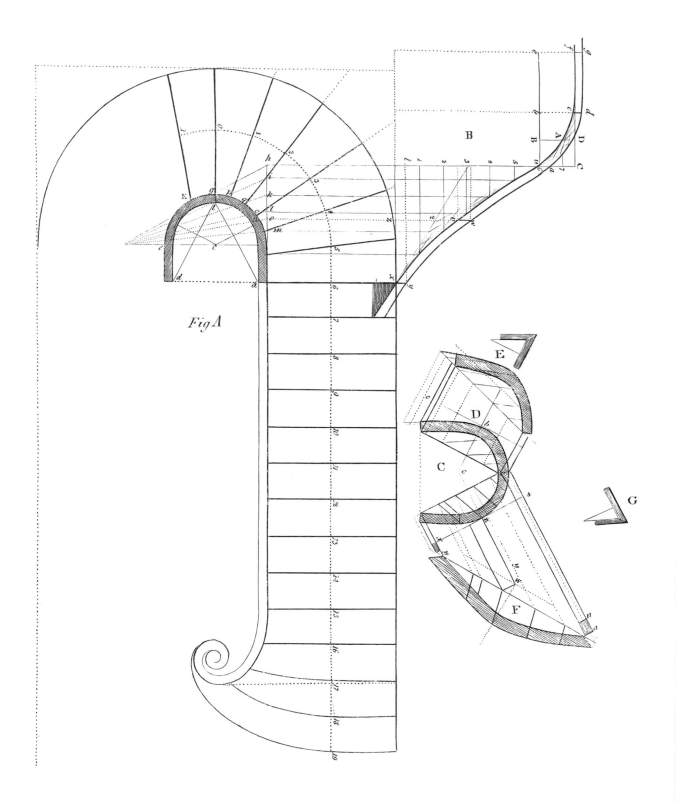

Fig A

B

C   D   E

F   G

PLATE L.

TO DIMINISH THE STEP OF A STAIR, WINDING ROUND ONE OF THE QUARTERS TO A
LEVEL LANDING.

Find the stretchout round half the circular part of the rail, as directed for the
foregoing plates, and complete the falling mould as directed in the last plate,
for the winding part of the rail, which is six steps from t to w; in order to bring
the rail with an easy turn round to the landing, set off the height to another step
from w to 7, and let the under edge of the rail be half the height of a step above
that to C; or it may be more according to the discretion of the workman; then
the rail will be half the height of a step more upon the landing, than it is upon
the winders; through C draw C f parallel to the base, and continue the line 2 u,
that forms the intersection below the winders up to D, and ease off the angle u
D c by intersecting lines, will give the under edge of the mould turning up to the
landing; in order that the last step beyond the quarter should follow the mould,
draw a line through 7, the height of the last step, parallel to u b, or C c, cutting
the underside of the falling mould at A; through A, draw A, B, parallel to C l;
then u B is the tread of the last step of the rail, which is set from g to E. The face
moulds at D and F are completed in the same manner as directed in the last
plate, and the moulds in plate 47; fig. D, is also laid down by the same method,
the height of the sections being taken from the falling mould that corresponds to
that place of the rail which the face mould is made for; and the bevels that are
laid down above each face mould will show how much you must bevel the edge
of your plank, before you can apply the face moulds to the plank; then draw
the plumb of your rail, upon the bevelled edge, by the other bevels that are
shown at the sections; then apply your mould to each side of the plank, keeping it fair with the bevelled edge, the same as in other cases before mentioned.

PLATE H.

EXPLANATION OF THE SOLIDS.

FIG. 1.

Shows the rail as completely squared upon a cylinder, with the plan of the hollow cylinder underneath from which the rail is formed.

FIG. 2.

Exhibits the manner in which the elevation of the helix or spiral line which forms one of the outside arrises of the rail is drawn.

Divide the exterior circle into any number of equal parts, or according to the number of steps : and divide the height, or part of the axis intended for one revolution, into the same number of equal parts ; draw lines through the points of division perpendicular to the axis ; and from the points of division in the exterior circle draw lines parallel to the said axis ; through every two corres-ponding points draw a curve *a b c*, &c. and this curve will form one of the arris lines as represented in *fig.* 1.

The same curve may be repeated in as many equal heights as the revolutions are in number.

This will give some idea of the rail according to the definition I have given of it.

Though the figure here exhibited for a rail in the square is supposed to be cut out of a hollow cylinder in one entire piece, in order to convey more readily the idea of the helixal solid ; it is evident, however, that the square helix may be cut out of short pieces of wood, so that the fibres of the wood may run in any direction we please. Therefore, since we have this in our choice, the nearer the fibres run in the direction of the length of the piece, or to the arris lines of the helixal solid, the stronger it will be.

There are two different kinds of joints ; one is formed by planes parallel to the axis of the cylinder ; and the other by a plane perpendicular to one of the arris lines of the rail ; those joints that are formed by planes parallel to the axis of the cylinder, are called splice-joints ; and those joints that are formed by planes perpendicular to the arris lines, are called butt-joints.

Formation of the Solids.

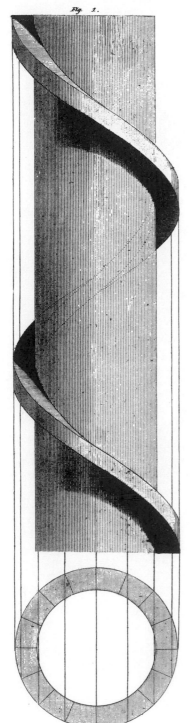

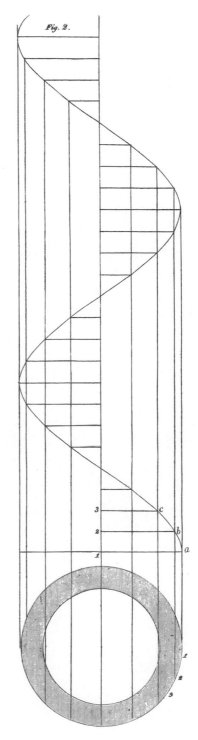

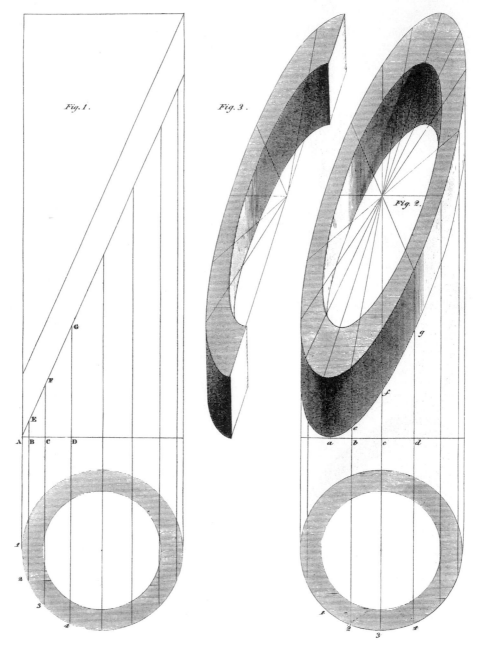

PLATE **I.**

Formation of the Solids.

Fig. 1.

Fig. 3.

Fig. 2.

PLATE I.

EXHIBITS A PORTION OF THE CYLINDROME CONTAINED BETWEEN TWO PARALLEL PLANES ; AND HERE THE CYLINDROME IS WHAT IS COMMONLY DENOTED A HOLLOW CYLINDER.

FIG. 1.

Shows the thickness of the portion, and the inclination of the cutting planes to the base, which cutting planes will form two equal and similar sections ; and as it is well known that the section of a cylinder is an ellipse, each section or face will be contained between two concentric and similar ellipses ; but it is obvious, that as the solid returns to itself, the entire helix cannot be made of so great a portion of the cylindrome, unless the cutting planes were extended to a very remote distance from each other ; and consequently the waste of wood would be very great. The solid here exhibited is therefore of no practical utility, but is absolutely necessary in theory, as an idea of the parts of any thing which are very dissimilar cannot easily be formed without having a correct idea of the whole.

FIG. 2.

The same portion of the cylindrome representing the solid obliquely, or as projected on a plane, in such a manner that another plane, which is perpendicular to the planes of the sections of the solid is neither parallel nor perpendicular to the plane of projection. This position presents the most correct idea of the real form of the solid to the imagination. One of the sectional sides is brought entirely to view, the other being concealed by the body itself ; and a portion of each of the curved sides is shown.

The method of representing such a solid will easily be found, by observing that the corresponding letters in the elevations, *figs.* 1 and 2, have equal heights, and the distances of the numerals on the plane are equal.

FIG. 3.

A representation of half the solid ; but even here the waste of wood would be too great ; and as the fibres of the wood are cut across on both sides, the piece would be too weak.

PLATE LI.

PLAN AND ELEVATION FOR A SMALL TOWN HOUSE.

No. 1.

Kitchen and cellar floor, twenty seven by twenty-five feet, from out to out.
  a Cellar, nine by twenty two feet.
  b Kitchen, sixteen by fifteen feet.
  c Kitchen closet, six feet square.

No. 2.

PARLOUR FLOOR.

d Parlour, sixteen feet square.
e Breakfast room, eight feet six inches by sixteen feet.
g China closet, six feet square.
f Front entry, eight feet six inches, by six feet.

No. 3.

Chamber floor, with the dimensions figured on the plate.

No. 4.

Upper chamber floor, with all the dimensions figured on the plate.

Plate 51.

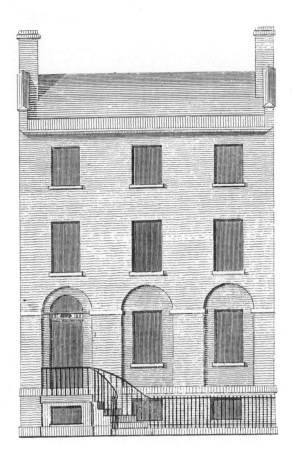

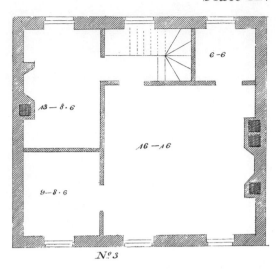

6 - 6

13 - 8 . 6

16 - 16

9 - 8 . 6

Nº 3

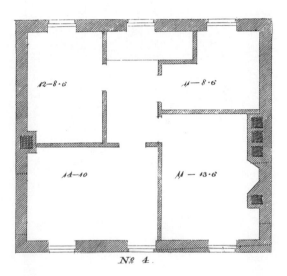

12 - 8 . 6

11 - 8 . 6

14 - 10

11 - 13 . 6

Nº 4.

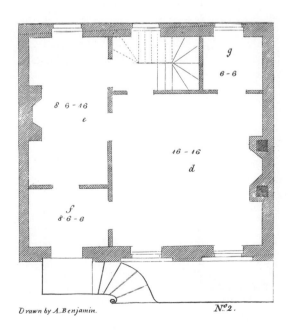

g
6 - 6

8 6 - 16
e

16 - 16
d

f
8 . 6 - 6

Drawn by A. Benjamin. Nº 2.

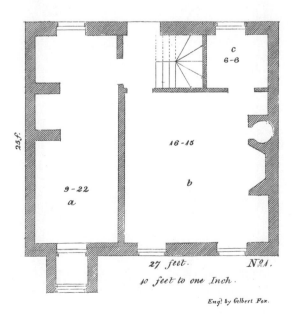

c
6 - 6

25 f.

16 - 15

9 - 22
a

b

27 feet. Nº 1.

10 feet to one Inch.

Eng.ᵗ by Gilbert Fox.

Plate **52**.

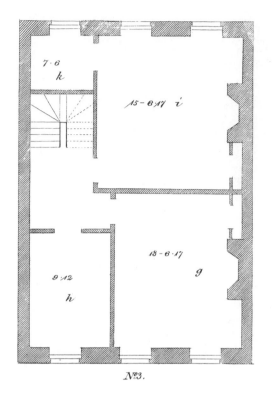

N.º3.

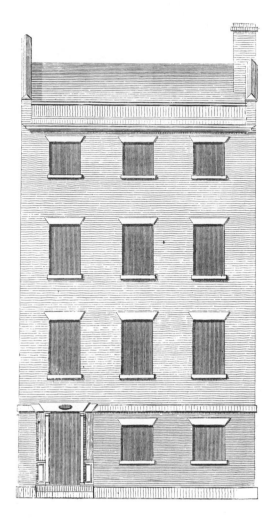

7·6

15 – 6 . 17

d

15 – 6 . 17

c

7 . square

e

Drawn by A.Benjamin. N.º 2

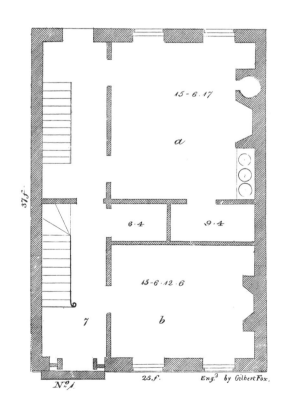

37.f.

15 – 6 . 17

a

6·4

9·4

15·6·12·6

b

7

N.º 1   25.f. Eng.ᵈ by Gilbert Fox.

PLATE LII.

PLAN AND ELEVATION FOR A TOWN HOUSE.

No. 1.

Basement story floor, twenty five by thirty seven feet.

a Kitchen, fifteen feet six inches by seventeen feet, in the clear.

b Breakfast or counting room, fifteen feet six inches by twelve feet six inches.

No. 2.

PARLOUR FLOOR.

c and *d*, Parlour and diningroom, fifteen feet six inches by seventeen feet.

f China closet, seven feet by six feet.

e Library, seven feet square.

No. 3.

CHAMBER FLOOR.

g Spare chamber, thirteen feet six inches, by seventeen feet.

i Lady's or gentleman's bedchamber, fifteen feet six inches by seventeen feet.

k Dressingroom, seven feet by six feet.

h Small bedchamber, nine feet by twelve feet.

Glass in basement story, eleven by seventeen inches, six lights each window. Principal floor, eleven by sixteen inches, twelve lights each window. Chamber floor, eleven by fifteen inches, twelve lights each window. Upper chamber floor, eleven by fifteen inches, nine lights each window.

26

PLATE LIII.

PLAN AND ELEVATION FOR A TOWN HOUSE.

No. 1.

Basement story floor, fifty four by thirty five feet.

a Hall, or principal entrance.
b Kitchen, twenty feet square.
c Office, eleven by twenty feet.
d Library, ten by twenty feet.

No. 2.

PARLOUR FLOOR.

f Diningroom, twenty by thirty feet, in the clear.
g Parlour, twenty feet square.
h Breakfastroom, eleven by eighteen feet.
i Pantry, or china closet, ten by eleven feet.

A, represents that part of the railing which is placed exactly over each window from *a* to *b*, is the width of the window ; from *b* to *c*, is a part of the panel and railing, which is placed over the peers, between windows.

Glass, in basement story, six lights in a window, of twelve and a half by twenty three inches. Principal floor, twelve and a half by twenty one inches ; twelve lights each window. Chamber story, twelve and a half by twenty inches ; twelve lights each window. Upper chamber floor, twelve and a half by nineteen inches ; nine lights each window.

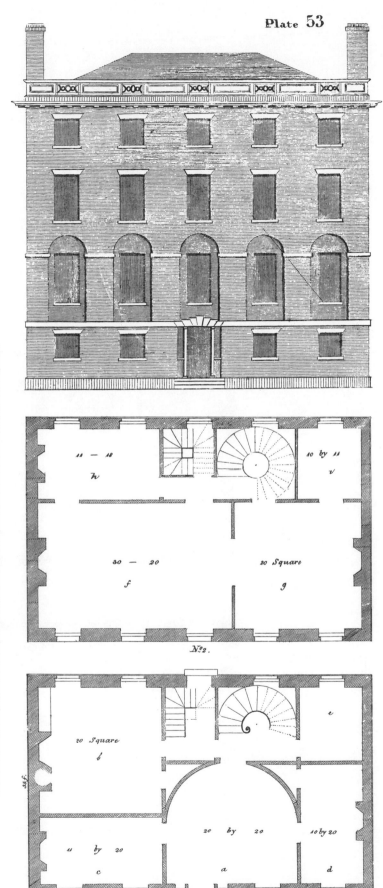

Plate 53

Scale 15 feet to one Inch

No.2.

No.1.

A.Benjamin Del.

Fox Sc.

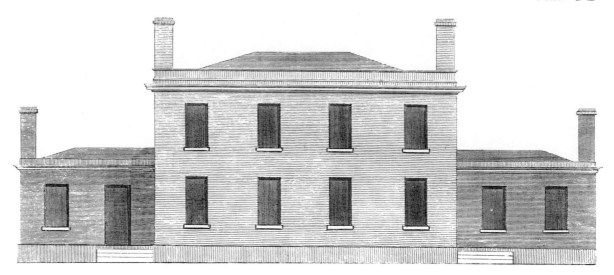

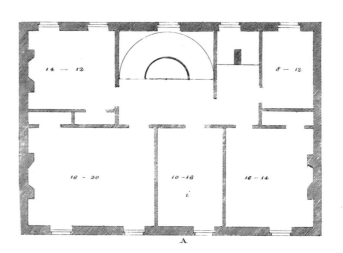

A

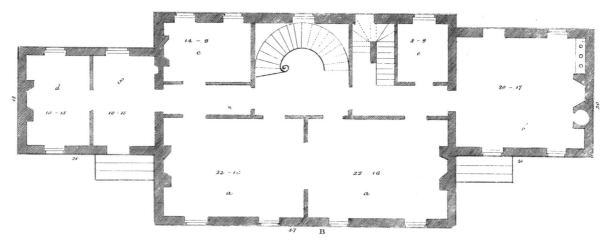

B

A. Benjamin Del.

Fox Sc.

PLATE LIV.

PLAN AND ELEVATION FOR A HOUSE WHICH IS INTENDED FOR A COUNTRY SITUATION.

No. 1.

Is the principal floor, forty seven by thirty three feet.

a a Parlour and diningroom, twenty two by sixteen feet, each.

b Kitchen, twenty by seventeen feet.

c Breakfastroom, nine by fourteen feet.

d Library, ten by fifteen feet.

Entry, ten by fifteen feet.

e Pantry or china closet, eight by nine feet.

No. 2.

Chamber floor, which contains five bedchambers.   The dimensions as on the plate.

PLATE LV.

DESIGNS FOR A HOUSE INTENDED FOR THE COUNTRY.

A, Basement story, forty seven by thirty feet, from out to out.

   c Kitchen, seventeen by twenty one feet.

   d Storeroom, ten by six feet.

   m Kitchen closet, four by sixteen feet.

P, Entry and back stairs.

f Cellar, seventeen feet square.

e Cellar, twenty two by ten feet.

n n n Foundation of steps.

B, Principal floor.

   i Parlour, seventeen by twenty one feet.

   k China closet, ten by six feet.

   l Back stairs and entry.

   h Front entry and stairway, nine feet wide.

   g Drawingroom, seventeen by twenty seven feet.

On the chamber floor may be four bedchambers, and on the attic floor three.

Plate 55.

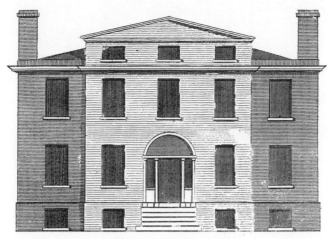

Scale 15 Feet to one Inch

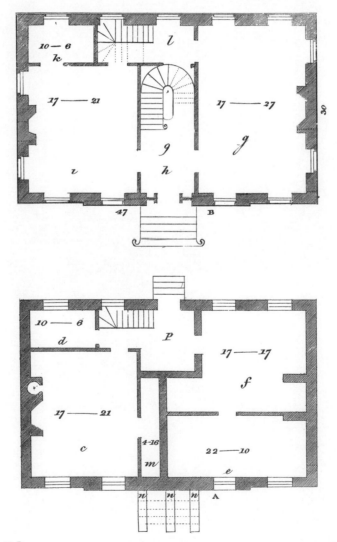

A. Benjamin Del.

G. Fox Sc.

Plate 56

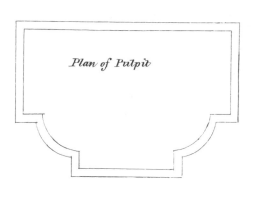

Plan of Pulpit

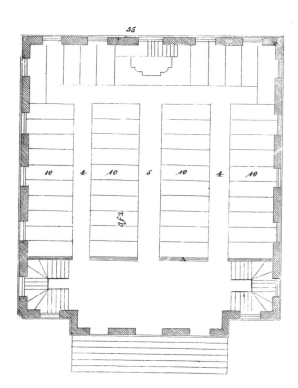

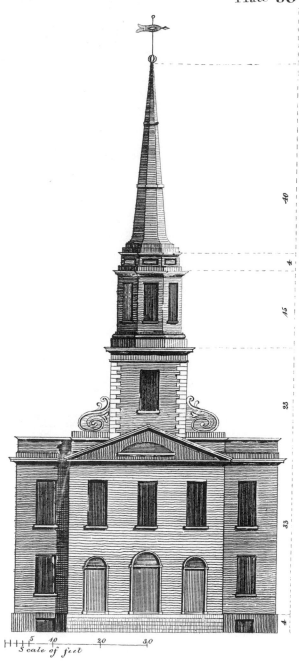

PLATE LVI.

PLAN AND ELEVATION FOR A MEETING-HOUSE,

Which contains fifty pews on the first floor, and will accommodate about four hundred people, which will be sufficiently large for most country parishes. The front of the front gallery, is intended to come exactly over the partition, A. The wall, including the eave cornice, is thirty three feet high. Make the eave cornice about one twenty eighth part of thirty three feet; make the cornice to the tower, about one twenty fifth part of the height, which is eleven inches ; make the cornice to the next story, which is an octagon, one twentieth part of the height, which is nine inches. The cornice B, on plate twenty seven, would be proper for the eave cornice ; and D, on plate twenty six, for the cornice to the tower. D, on plate twenty seven for the cornice to the next story.

The windows in the first story, are to contain twenty four panes of glass, of ten by fifteen inches ; second story, twenty eight panes of glass, ten by fifteen inches.—This house may be built of wood, and on account of its simple plainness, for a less sum of money, than houses of this sort usually are built.

27

PLATE LVII.

PLAN AND ELEVATION FOR A MEETING HOUSE.

This plan was copied from the original drawing, which was made for the congregational meeting-house at West Boston.   The size of the house is seventy five feet square ; porch, twenty by forty six feet ; to contain one hundred and twelve pews on the lower floor.   The gallery is supported by columns of the Composite order.   The ceiling has a dome in the centre, of forty two feet in diameter, which rises six feet ; the level parts of the ceiling, are ornamented with sunk panels.

The eave cornice is taken from B, on plate twenty six, and is one twenty eighth part of the height.   The third story of the porch is proportioned exactly after the Doric order.   The cornice to the attic story is about one seventeenth part of the height, and is taken from D, on plate twenty seven.   The cupola has the proportions of the Ionic order.   The windows in the first story contain twenty four panes of glass, of eleven by fifteen inches.   Windows of the second story, contain twenty eight panes of glass, of eleven by sixteen inches.   Windows in the third story of the porch contain twenty eight panes of glass, eleven by fifteen inches, with circular heads.   Attic story, six panes eleven by eighteen inches.

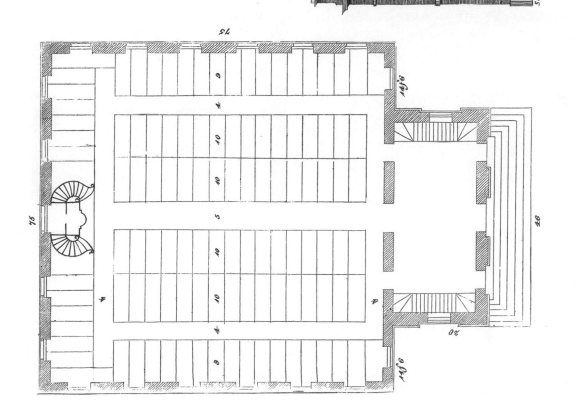

Plate **57**

Scale 80 feet to one Inch.

Wightman Sc.

A Bayannin Del.

Plate 58

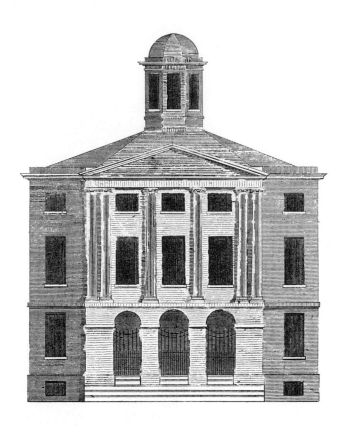

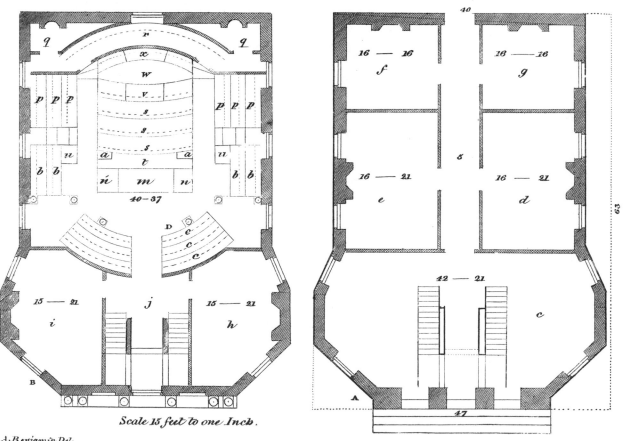

Scale 15 feet to one Inch.

A. Benjamin Del.

PLATE LVIII.

PLAN AND ELEVATION FOR A COURT-HOUSE.

A, Plan of first floor.

d Clerk's office, sixteen by twenty one feet.

e Room for grand jury, sixteen by twenty one feet.

g Register of deeds' office, sixteen feet square.

f Probate court, sixteen feet square.

c Hall and stairway, forty two by twenty one feet.

B, Plan of the second floor.

D, Courtroom, forty by thirty seven feet.

r Judges' seat.

q q Small lobbies.

x Clerk's seat.

W Table.

v Attorney general's seat.

s s s Attorney's seats.

p p p p p p Jury seats.

w w Sheriff boxes.

t Passage between attorney's seats and bar.

n n Constable's boxes.

m Bar.

a a Stand for witnesses.

j Stairway.

h and *i* Juryrooms, fifteen by twenty one feet each.

b b b b Seats for witnesses.

Over h and i may be two lobbies, about fifteen by seventeen feet each ; and, over the circular seats c c c, a gallery which will contain about one hundred people.   It is intended to have a dome in the ceiling over the courtroom, of thirty feet diameter, and to rise above the horizontal ceiling five feet.

PLATE K.

PLAN AND ELEVATION OF A CHURCH.

Plate K, fig. a, is a plan ; fig. b, an elevation of a Church, drawn on a scale of twenty feet to an inch, which will contain about one thousand people.   The dotted line on the plan represents the front line of the gallery, which is intended to run across the front only, and not continue along the sides of the house, as is common in churches in this country.

PLATE L.

Plate L, fig. c, is a side elevation for the same building.   Fig. d represents a plan of the cupola ; 1, shews the shape and size of the tower, as it rises from the roof of the house ; 2, the shape and size of the story which is intended to contain the bell and clock ; 3, the shape and size of the octagon story, which is to be finished after the Ionic order ; and 4, the size and shape of the base which is to support the roof, e shows the size and shape of the glass, and the manner of finishing the inside of one of the windows, any part of which may be measured by the scale of feet below it.

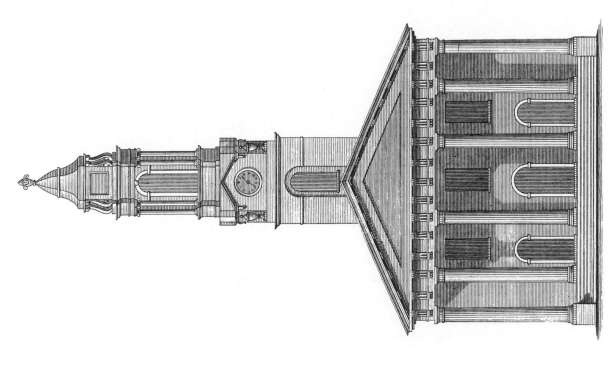

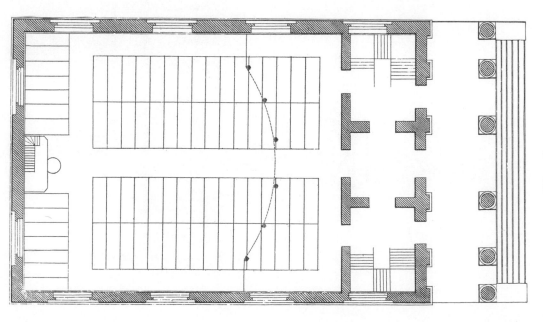

Plate L.

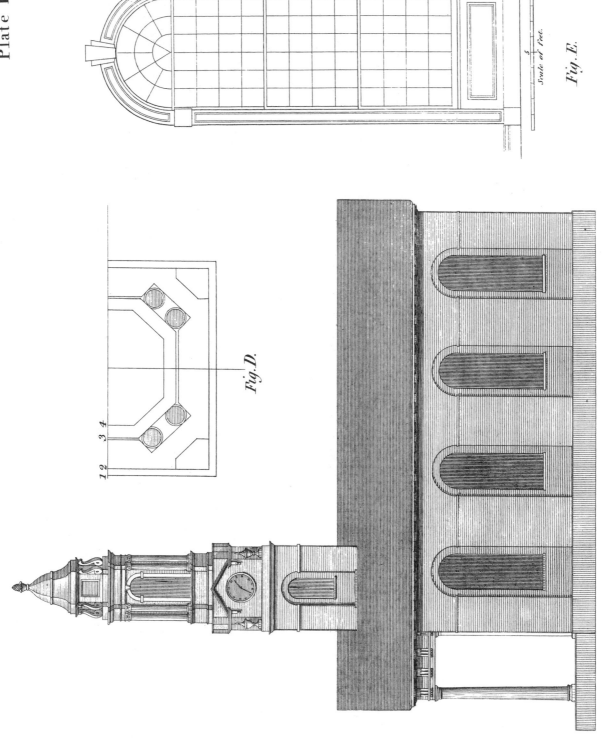

Fig. E.

Scale of Feet.

Fig. D.

Fig. C.

OBSERVATIONS

ON BUILDING OF HOUSES, TO ELUCIDATE THE PRECEDING PLANS, AND ASSIST THE STUDENT IN THE PRACTICAL PARTS.

THE first thing to be done in planning a house, is to know the wants of the person who is to occupy it ; the next to know the situation of the ground it is to cover ; then to take into consideration the number, size, and height of the rooms wanted ; also, proper convenient stairs, entries, passages, &c. Let the kitchen be situated, so as to have as easy a communication with the dining and breakfastrooms as possible ; let the pantry or china closet communicate with the diningroom by a door, and with the passage from the kitchen by a door or window. Place the door in such a manner as to make the distance from one part of the house to the other, as short as possible ; still keep uniformity in view, as it is one of the greatest beauties in architecture ; yet convenience ought not to make too great a sacrifice to it. The eye ought to see, at the same time, every part of the building, and be sure that no one part of it interferes with another ; also, to see that the rooms are properly lighted, and at the same time, that there are a sufficient number of windows, and of a size suitable for the external part of the building.

Strength, convenience, and beauty, are the principal things to be attended to. To have strength, there must be a good solid foundation ; and never place piers over openings of windows or doors. Openings of windows or doors in different stories, ought to be exactly perpendicular, one over the other. Care ought to be taken, not to place heavy girders or beams over doors or windows, or to lay timber of any kind under fireplaces. As to the proportion of windows to rooms, I do not believe any certain determined rule can be given for their height and breadth, although there are several European writers, who have given rules for their proportion. I think Sir William Chambers has given the best proportion of any one I have seen, yet I do not find it to answer in all

cases ; he adds the depth and the height of the rooms on the principal floor to·
gether, and takes one eighth part thereof for the width of the window.   The
width and height of doors, depends on the size and height of rooms in some
degree, although there is not any room so small as not to require a door sufficiently large for a person to pass through its opening.   In the course of my
own practice, I have made doors for rooms of sixteen by eighteen or twenty
feet, and ten feet high, three feet wide, and seven feet or seven feet two inches
high.   When rooms have been twenty by twenty three or twenty four feet, and
twelve or fourteen feet high, I have made the doors three feet six or seven
inches wide, and seven feet eight inches, or eight feet high ; all the doors in the
same room ought to be of the same size, except where two doors are placed
together between the two principal rooms, which are called folding doors.
They ought to be made from eight to twelve inches higher than the other doors
of the room, or they will, on account of their width, appear to be lower than the
others ; these folding doors are commonly used in Boston, and are very convenient, particularly so when placed between small rooms, both for the circulation
of air, when windows and doors are opened, and for the reception of large
companies.

The size of the outside doors, must be governed by the building in which
they are placed.   If in a town house with a narrow front and small windows
on each side, like plate fifty two, three feet four or six inches will do very well
for its width, but if wanted for a large house, and without side lights, it ought
to be made much wider ; say from three feet ten inches to four feet ; and in
some cases, four feet four or six inches wide, and never less than two diameters high.

The chimney ought not to project into the room more than from fifteen to
twenty inches if it can be avoided, and care should be taken to place them on
the most convenient side of the room.   For size of fireplaces, see explanation
of chimney-pieces.   Never make the funnel less than twelve inches square,
and if there is sufficient room sixteen inches is a good size where a fireplace is
about four feet between the jambs.

Plate 59.

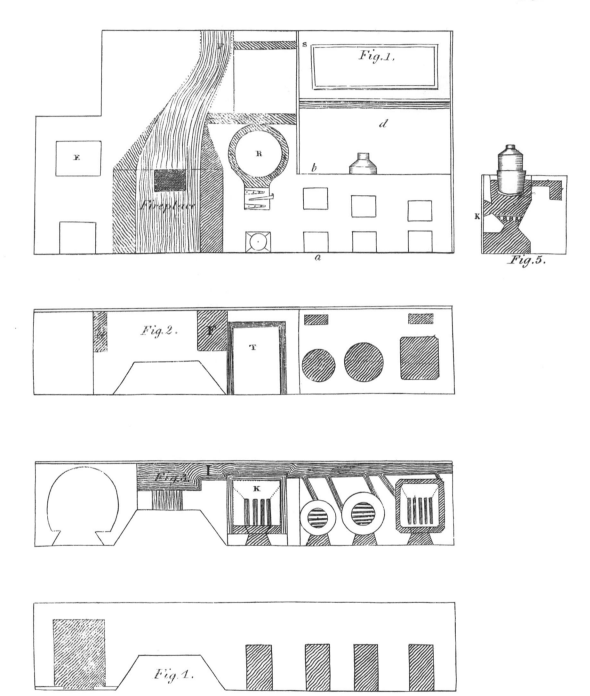

Fig.1.

Fig.5.

Fig.2.

Fig.3.

Fig.4.

PLATE LIX.

METHOD OF BUILDING KITCHEN FIREPLACES WITH RUMFORD'S ROASTERS AND BOILERS.

FIG. 1.

Represents a front view or elevation of a kitchen fireplace, common brick oven, Rumford roaster and doors to the boilers.

N. B. The height of this brick work from the hearth a, to the top b, is two feet ten inches.

The space above the boilers d, represents a sliding shutter, hanging by weights, to slide up and down, and close in the steam of the boilers.

S, at the dotted lines, is the passage for the steam to go off into the chimney.

R, represents the front of the roaster, with its flues for the smoke to pass round the cylinder into the chimney.

E, represents the front of the oven.

FIG. 2.

Represents boilers with the brick work closed round the rims, and two stoppers for clearing out the soot of the canal.

F, in fig. 1 and 2, represents flue of fireplace.

G, flue of oven.

T, inside of roaster with its flues ; mark out the dot at the back end where the steam tube comes in.

FIG. 3.

Represents the flues of the boilers passing into the canal, at the level of K, in fig. 5.

I, is the canal for smoke to pass into the chimney.

K, represents the grate of the roaster, the dotted lines from the grate represent the rising of the brick work to the back of the roaster.

FIG. 4.

Is the ground plan of fireplace and ashpits.

FIG. 5.

Represents the inside section of the thirteen and a half inch boiler, with its steam dish and cover; on the descent from door to grate is one and a half inches.

GENERAL OBSERVATIONS.

Eight or nine inches ought to be allowed from the top of the grates to the bottom of the boilers, the distance between the fire and ashpit door may vary according to the depth of the boilers, as appears in fig. 1.

Make the space between the grates and bottom of the roaster not less than one foot; the distance between the fire and ash door may be from two to five bricks, as is most convenient; the space round the roaster for the smoke, two and a half inches; round the boilers, two inches.

In small boilers one brick will be sufficient to cover the flues; but in large ones, such as washkettles, they ought to be covered with two.

Make the small flues that lead from the boilers, two inches high and three long. The main canal ought to be from eight to twelve inches deep, below the bottom of the small ones.

Where it can conveniently be done, it is best to lead the smoke of the roaster down as low as the top of the bottom shelf, which will greatly assist in retaining the heat.

NOTE. This plate was drawn by Mr. Lancaster, who has been more successful in *setting* Rumford's roasters and boilers, than any other person; and was explained by him and Mr. Howe, who is the only one that *makes* them in Boston.

INDEX.